Diane Maddex

Photographs by Alexander Vertikoff

Harry N. Abrams, Inc., Publishers

Bungalow Nation

Dedicated to Robert Winter,
a bungalow lover who has helped spark
our modern love affair with these endearing houses

Editorial Concept: Diane Maddex and Richard Olsen
Produced by Archetype Press, Inc.
Project Director: Diane Maddex
Research Assistant: Robert L. Maddex
Designer: Robert L. Wiser

This book was composed in Monotype Italian Oldstyle, a serif typeface de-signed in 1893 by Joseph W. Phinney for American Type Founders. Origi-nally named Jenson Oldstyle, it was patterned after William Morris's Golden Type of 1890. The display typography is Britannic, a bold sans-serif type-face released by Stephenson Blake in 1905.

Illustration and Text Credits
Case binding: Pillows with an Arts and Crafts–style dragonfly motif inspired by the "play impulse" described in Ernest Batchelder's *Design in Theory and Practice,* 1910. Courtesy Dianne Ayres, Arts and Crafts Period Textiles (www.textilestudio.com). Endpapers: "In the Land of the Bungalow," George F. Devereaux, Los Angeles, 1929. Courtesy Robert Winter. Page 1: From Henry L. Wilson, *A Short Sketch of the Evolution of the Bungalow,* ca. 1920s. Reprint, Dover Publications, 1993. Pages 2–3: Stucco and shingle bun-galow on North Holliston Avenue in Pasadena's Bungalow Heaven. Pasadena Museum of History Archives. Pages 11, 13, 14: Verses from "The Bungalow," published in *Keith's Magazine,* April 1915. Pages 12–13 (all): Pasadena Mu-seum of History Archives. Page 23: From Henry L. Wilson, *A Short Sketch of the Evolution of the Bungalow.* Pages 32–33 (top): Pasadena Museum of His-tory Archives. Page 32 (bottom): Curt Teich Postcard Archives, Lake County (Ill.) Discovery Museum. Pages 64–67: Courtesy the Gamble House, Pasadena. Pages 78–79 (top): Manuscripts, Special Collections, University Archives, University of Washington Libraries, SMR 231. Pages 116–17 (top): Minnesota Historical Society. Page 168: Michael Williams. Pages 196–97 (top): Alexandria (Va.) Library, Local History–Special Collections; (bottom left and right) author's collection.

The following photographs by Alexander Vertikoff are used courtesy *Ameri-can Bungalow* magazine: Pages 14–15, 16–17, 21 (bottom left and right), 22 (top), 33 (bottom), 34–35, 68–71, 72, 74–75, 100–3, 110–11, 112–13, 120–21, 158–59, 169–71, 186–87.

Library of Congress Cataloging-in-Publication Data
Maddex, Diane.
Bungalow nation / by Diane Maddex; photography by Alexander Vertikoff ; foreword by Richard Moe.—1st ed.
p. cm.
Includes bibliographical references.
ISBN 0-8109-4628-9 (alk. paper)
1. Bungalows—United States. 2. Interior decoration—United States—His-tory—20th century. 3. Arts and crafts movement—United States—Influence. I. Vertikoff, Alexander. II. Title.
NA7571.M33 2003
728'.373'0973—dc21
2003004496

Printed and bound in Singapore

10   9   8   7   6   5   4   3   2

Harry N. Abrams, Inc.
100 Fifth Avenue
New York, N.Y. 10011
www.abramsbooks.com

Abrams is a subsidiary of

LA MARTINIÈRE
GROUPE

Contents

Foreword

I f one were to compile a list of this country's most numerous and most widespread residential building types, the bungalow would surely vie for a top spot. What accounts for the bungalow's popularity? Marketing certainly played an important role. Bungalows were displayed prominently in the pages of popular magazines such as the *Ladies' Home Journal,* and influential editors extolled the large windows, airy porches, built-in furnishings, open floor plans, and other features that made bungalows convenient and healthful. Affordability and ease of construction were also major factors. Their use of natural materials and lack of fussy ornamentation placed bungalows within the price range of a large audience of would-be homeowners.

But in the final analysis, bungalows proliferated simply because people liked them. This helps explain the enduring popularity of these structures. Read the homeowners' comments that appear in this book, and you'll find them referring again and again to their deep affection for their houses, an affection sparked and nourished by the blend of easy comfort and unique style that has always made a well-built bungalow feel like the very embodiment of home.

Long taken for granted, bungalows are now back in the spotlight. First-time home buyers, like their predecessors almost a century ago, are drawn to bungalows' historic charm and relative affordability. Architectural historians are documenting the wide range of substyles and regional variations embraced by the term *bungalow.* And preservationists are recognizing that bungalows tell an important part of America's story and are worthy of our best efforts to save and celebrate them.

Naturally, I am pleased to see bungalows in the Twin Cities (where I spent many years) and Washington (where I now live) highlighted in this book—but I know that Diane Maddex's words and Alexander Vertikoff's photographs will resonate with readers everywhere. I urge everyone to join us in working to preserve these modest landmarks that constitute both a valuable housing resource and a unique—and uniquely beloved—part of America's rich heritage.

—*Richard Moe, President*
National Trust for Historic Preservation

This handsome bungalow in Takoma Park, Maryland, built about 1921, was rescued from years of neglect by the local developer Art McMurdie. An artist now makes her home here, working in a studio added onto the back together with a kitchen and a master bedroom above. The view from the back porch looks like countryside (above). Atop the sloping shed roof, a large gabled dormer invites sunshine into the surprisingly roomy upper story (opposite).

Preface

My first memory as a child is lodged in the snowy front yard of a sturdy bungalow outside Washington, D.C., where I helped my mother and older sister build a beret-topped snowman. Coming from Riverside, California, my family felt lucky in the pinched postwar housing market to have found a broad gabled roof over our heads in suburban Hyattsville, Maryland, and a generous porch to play on. Because we soon moved on to other homes and other neighborhoods in the capital area, the memory of that bungalow, if not the snowy yard, faded over the years. Even as I celebrated bungalows in the 1990s by producing *American Bungalow Style* with Robert Winter and Alexander Vertikoff, it never entered my consciousness that I myself had once lived in a bungalow.

As I began working on this second bungalow tribute, a childhood photo album prepared for me by my mother brought all those memories flooding back. Not only was there the Hyattsville bungalow where this California girl relished her first snowfall; my Chicago grandmother had also spent her last years in a sunny Spanish bungalow on a tropical street in Hollywood—my favorite place to visit. My younger sister began married life in a tiny bungalow, most likely ordered long before from Sears, at the bottom of a hill in Takoma Park, Maryland, another D.C. suburb. My husband's great uncle built one of the few bungalows, an expansive brick example, in the colonial-era town of Shepherdstown, West Virginia, where the Federal style is by far the norm.

Bungalow stories like these can be found almost everywhere. Perhaps it is the architecture lover's version of "six degrees of separation": is there anyone who doesn't know someone who has lived in a bungalow or someone who knows someone else who has? Given how many bungalows were built in the early twentieth century in just about every small town and big American city, we are indeed an interlocked bungalow nation. This book that Alex Vertikoff and I have assembled is an album of stories and memories like the photo album divulging the bungalow in my own past. The subjects here for the most part are not architectural landmarks in which elaborate porticoes or imposing pedigrees tell the main tale. The stories these bungalows relate are full of families and lives led over the past century—and still being lived in and dearly loved today.

Chicago bungalow owners keep an eye on their neighborhoods through Prairie-style art glass windows, such as this gracefully arched design.

Our examples could have come from just about any place in the United States—from Bellingham, Washington; Portland, Oregon; San Diego or Ontario, California; Glendale, Arizona; Roswell, New Mexico; Wichita Falls, Texas; Topeka, Kansas; Mobile, Alabama; Tampa, Florida; Atlanta or Macon, Georgia; Asheville, North Carolina; Bowling Green or Lexington, Kentucky; Atlantic City, New Jersey; Buffalo, New York; Portsmouth, New Hampshire; Milwaukee or Madison, Wisconsin—any of the thousands of towns where bungalows remain proud neighbors. Instead we selected five cities and their environs to represent this vast bungalow nation of ours: Los Angeles and Pasadena, Seattle, Minneapolis and St. Paul, Chicago, and Washington, D.C. In these places are bungalow stories similar to those found in neighborhoods coast to coast.

Alex Vertikoff and I are grateful most of all to the more than seventy-five homeowners who invited us into their homes and shared their love of bungalows. We hope that we have captured even a small part of the pride they show in their homes. John Brinkmann, founder and publisher of *American Bungalow* magazine, has once again been a trusted supporter and adviser, including recommending Tim Counts in the Twin Cities and Michael Williams in Chicago, both dedicated bungalow owners featured in the book who offered invaluable assistance in locating bungalows in their cities and shepherding the photographer.

Other individuals also provided assistance, for all of which we are indebted. In Los Angeles: Tim Andersen, Ken Miedema, Nancy Phillips, and John Ripley. In Seattle: Karen Hovde, Lawrence Kreisman of Historic Seattle, Larry Johnson and Howard Miller, and Laurie Taylor. In the Twin Cities: Kristi Lee Johnson, Dennie Juillert and Kevin Thompson, Tracy Smith, and Dennis R. Williams. In Chicago: Bonita Mall, Paul and Amy Mattar, Dominic A. Pacyga, Ashish and Colleen Taylor Sen, and Charles Shanabruch. In Washington, D.C.: Caroline Alderson, Mary Anne O'Boyle Leary, Eileen McGuckian of Peerless Rockville, William J. Murtagh, Loretta Neumann, Carol T. Peters, Pamela Scott, Katherine Holt Springston, Sally Sims Stokes, and Dwight Young. And for his evocative photographs, we are all grateful to Alex Vertikoff.

—*Diane Maddex*

IN THE LAND OF THE BUNGALOW

England may no longer be a nation of shopkeepers, but America remains a nation of bungalow owners. The twentieth century began and ended with a rush to secure a bungalow of one's own, a cozy home in which to find old-fashioned values of family, simplicity, economy, craftsmanship, and a life lived in harmony with nature. Newspaper advertisements placed by Fannie Mae to promote the "American Dream of homeownership" still show a bungalow as the archetype of home, or at least of a starter home. Hollywood filmmakers scout out bungalows as props standing in for the American home in Anywhere, U.S.A. Books and even a magazine devoted to bungalows encourage this dream alongside pointers on how to restore everything from natural colors to period kitchens. A century has passed, but we remain a bungalow nation.

> **"Among the shrubbery and shade trees**
> **The brisk little bungalow stands. . . ."**

The first documented reference to an American bungalow, describing a rambling summer cottage with a wraparound veranda on Cape Cod, came in 1880. Four years later Arnold Brunner, an architect in New York, compiled a book of cottage designs that opened with a house closer to what we now recognize as a bungalow. "'Bungalows,' as the one storey houses used in India are called, seem adapted to some parts of America particularly as summer cottages," he noted.

As Brunner was clearly aware, the bungalow had made its way from India via England and had gained common parlance as a carefree cottage removed from everyday life. For more than a century earlier, British traders and colonists in India, looking for something to keep them out of the midday sun, had transformed native peasant huts that were

Designers of California bungalows had at their disposal a plenitude of native materials from wood to stone. For the Parsons House of 1910, built in Pasadena and later moved to Altadena, Arthur and Alfred Heineman used a descending scale of large boulders, redwood shingles, and gleaming oak interior details to mark the transition from outside in.

called *banggolos* into their own hybrid shelters. These one-story tent-like structures of unbaked brick, raised on a low foundation and shaded by a pyramidal roof of thatch called *bangla* (after Bengal), typically had a central living room surrounded by an airy veranda. They arose as temporary utilitarian concessions to living in an exotic tropical land, but the Anglicized name *bungalow* survived. Returning residents and travelers helped familiarize Britons with the word and the form. By 1869 bungalows, the name now implying leisure and low cost, were starting to pop up in British seaside resorts. Before long the idea of the bungalow traveled across the Atlantic.

Here the bungalow became synonymous mainly with escape—until it collided with the most persuasive housing reform movement the nation has ever seen. Brunner published his book of designs expressly to meet "a demand for dwellings reasonable in cost yet artistic and home-like." Although he and others were promoting summer cottages for the leisure class, the call for simple, artistic, homey, modern dwellings soon resonated throughout the land. A distaste for soulless industrialization and cheap gimcracks had rallied proponents of what came to be known as the Arts and Crafts movement in Britain. "Have nothing in your houses that you do not know to be useful, or believe to be beautiful," admonished William Morris (1834–96), the acknowledged leader, in 1882. Fellow proponents urged a return to old values linking crafts-manship with morality, a beautiful home with a beautiful heart.

In the United States the call for reform of society by way of housing was heeded by people as disparate as social workers, labor unionists, feminists, architects, artisans, and a furniture maker outside Syracuse, New York. Assuming Morris's mantle in America, Gustav Stickley (1858–1942) gave a national voice to localized choruses calling for an end to ostentatious, allegedly unhealthy Victorian houses in favor of simpler, artistic ones reflecting democratic middle-class values. "Even when attitudes about the family or about art or democracy were vague, contradictory, or self-serving, they nonetheless constituted an impor-tant set of shared issues for Americans," observes Gwendolyn Wright in *Moralism and the Model Home* about the rush toward reform.

Stickley's chief vehicle was a monthly magazine named *The Craftsman,* launched in October 1901 to propound "the ideals of honesty of mate-rials, solidity of construction, utility, adaptability to place, and aesthetic

Bungalow courts were the ultimate in democratic bungalow living. The prolific Arthur and Alfred Heineman of Pasadena designed both Alexandria Court (1914)—as architecturally exotic as its name—(top and bottom left) and this 1910 duplex at Los Robles Court (bottom right).

effect." Within three years he began to offer house plans that suited his Craftsman principles. Among the two hundred choices of all sizes offered over a dozen years were numerous bungalows. Stickley set out to Americanize the import, refashioning second homes "of extreme simplicity, of economic construction and intended for more or less primitive living" to meet their potential in the war on outmoded houses. Legions of entrepreneurs, designers, and builders followed suit.

"Its windows so clear and so gleaming Look out with suggestions of pride. . . ."

Between 1903, when the term *Craftsman bungalow* entered the lexicon, and 1905, when *California bungalow* joined it, the bungalow went from being a summer refuge with amorphous features to a house type with nearly universally recognized attributes: one or one and one-half stories with a low, sloping roof, an open plan inside, and a front porch tying it to nature. In *The American Bungalow, 1880–1930,* Clay Lancaster suggests that from the early 1900s into the 1930s, bungalows exceeded the number of cottages built in the country's previous 125 years. "Here resides the true importance of the bungalow: its quick rise to prominence, its nationwide expansion, and its overwhelming numbers," he notes. Bungalows enabled the middle class to move out of congested urban areas into an affordable paradise of their own. They were so popular that bungalow courts, schools, churches, and fire stations were built. Songs about bungalows added a lyrical note to the nation's small-house mania. America's love affair with the bungalow stemmed from "the idea that simplicity and artistry could be in harmony," says Robert Winter in *The California Bungalow.* "Only rarely in all of history has architecture been found outside the realm of 'the rich, the few, and the well-born.'" The bungalow, he concludes, "filled more than the need for shelter. It provided psychic fulfillment of the American Dream."

The lowly bungalow in fact became America's first national house type. Inexpensive, simple to build, modern, and sited on a private plot of land, it was architecture for a democracy as envisioned by Frank Lloyd Wright in 1910: "America, more than any other nation, presents a new architectural proposition, her ideal is democracy." For *The Craftsman,* it was "a house reduced to its simplest form where life can be carried on with the greatest amount of freedom." Not only did the bungalow supplant formal styles imported from abroad, it also insinuated itself into just about every city and hamlet across the nation. "Much more than the earlier American cottage, it was devoid of regional variation," suggests Anthony D. King in *The Bungalow.* "All over North America, the bungalow replaced distinctive regional types." Local building traditions and materials nonetheless produced local variants, as can be seen in the examples that follow. *E pluribus unum,* out of many, one.

The bungalow took root in southern California but quickly became the preferred housing for any streetcar suburb—reversing traditional patterns of cultural diffusion and thereby sealing the Golden State's status as a social innovator. California had the perfect soil in which to grow bungalows: a warm climate, a bursting population in need of housing, cheap land, and bold developers. Here as in other regions suburbanization was already under way, facilitated by trains, trolleys, and later cars that drove the middle class out of town and into a hoped-for arcadia.

"Here neighborly spirits shine clearly
And family life is implied...."

Bungalows designed for California's outdoor lifestyle eventually appeared in cities as different as Washington, D.C. Word traveled fast, helped along by a vast network of informers. Foremost among these were wish books of plans offered by promoters such as Gustav Stickley, who caught the California bug after a visit in 1904; Henry L. Wilson, Los Angeles's "Bungalow Man"; Henry H. Saylor; William P. Comstock; and William A. Radford. For as little as $5, would-be homeowners could purchase complete sets of plans and specifications and erect the bungalow of their choice. New nationwide shelter magazines such as *Ladies' Home Journal* and *House Beautiful* actively promoted the new ideals of house and home, backed up by *The Craftsman* from 1901 to 1916 and targeted periodicals such as *Bungalow Magazine* from 1909 to 1918. Newspapers and regional builders' magazines also spread the word, ensuring that the clone of a bungalow built first in Los Angeles might end up in Seattle or Alexandria, Virginia. Further carpeting the

Breakfast nooks like this perfect example in Tim Counts's Minneapolis kitchen were a staple in bungalows coast to coast. They could be ordered from builders' catalogues along with a host of other built-in features.

country with bungalows were mail-order companies that offered house kits ready to assemble. Sears, Montgomery Ward, Aladdin, Gordon Van-Tine, Lewis Homes, and others all made bungalows a mainstay among their ready-to-assemble houses. By being able to choose their own house designs in large numbers, average Americans exerted a stronger influence on their environment than they have any time since.

With few exceptions, these bungalows came from the drawing boards of anonymous architects. Some California designers caught the bungalow spirit. Practitioners such as Sylvanus Marston and Arthur and Alfred Heineman brought pride to the task, and a few others added a bungalow to their portfolios. In Seattle Ellsworth Storey produced distinctive bungalow designs, but elsewhere most important architects could not be bothered. After all, a bungalow could be ordered by mail.

By the 1920s, at the peak of bungalow building, the term that had inspired a movement began to lose its allure. When Woodrow Wilson derisively called Warren Harding "bungalow minded," it was clear that the bloom was off the bungalow. As period revival styles, Moderne apartments, and ranch houses took over as the preferred new places to live, however, bungalow families settled into their snug harbors and got on with life. Many of them never moved; other owners modified their bungalows to keep up with the times, often obliterating the welcoming wood and the cozy hearths that had made them so appealing in the first place.

Not until bungalows were inching toward their centennial mark did preservationists and buyers take notice of these houses that had comfortably settled into the national background. Renewed interest in the Arts and Crafts movement reactivated attention for these small offshoots as well. *American Bungalow* magazine, founded in 1990, now speaks to a new generation of "bungalovers" who have their own stories to tell. In our bungalow nation today—to paraphrase the words of Garrison Keillor, one of the Twin Cities' favorite sons—all the features are strong, all the materials are good looking, and all the bungalows are above average. Each one, like the residents of Lake Wobegon, remains a hardy citizen in our architectural democracy.

BUNGALOW STYLE

We all know one when we see it. There is a certain something, a few style markers—a "bungalogic" perhaps—that signal its presence, however its particular features are arranged in one region or another. Nestled under a low roof with wide overhangs, the exterior conveys a sense of simplicity and repose. Exposed rafter tails speak of structural honesty. A porch mediates between outdoors and in, while natural materials, natural colors, and an overriding horizontality link the house to the earth. The real domestic revolution was won inside, with labor-saving devices to please her and modern heating, plumbing, and electrical systems to satisfy him. The plan is compact yet open, with spaces flowing around natural dividers. The hearth, built of rustic brick or stone, takes center stage. Wood tones predominate, thanks to built-ins around the fireplace, in the dining room, and along the kitchen walls. The blocky wooden profiles of the furnishings echo the design choices of the builder or architect. But a bungalow's universal characteristic is that it is no bigger than it needs to be—whether less than 1,000 square feet, 1,500, or 2,500—and thus affordable, even if some joke that it is "a house that looks as if it had been built for less money than it actually cost."

Once California fleshed out the domestic dreams of trendsetters such as Gustav Stickley and gave the country a new type of house, the "bungle-oh" was transformed in its voyage across the continent. The Pacific Northwest adopted a pared-down Craftsman look and substituted its plentiful Douglas fir for redwood. The Twin Cities moved the focus inside, to escape the unforgiving weather, while Chicago followed Prairie School innovators and found a new way of building an inexpensive cottage. The nation's capital, voting on the myriad style choices, opted for some of each. "With the bungalow, as with no other house type," concludes John Brinkmann, publisher of *American Bungalow* magazine, "it is not so much the style that appeals as the *spirit.*"

The living room of Michael Williams and Karen Burke's classic Chicago bungalow is a showcase of bungalow style. Like enthroned royalty, the brick fireplace is recessed under an arch. Facing the Arts and Crafts settle are chairs that may be from Charles Stickley. The lighting complements the art glass windows—Chicago's own bungalow jewels.

Outside: The Natural House

"And my blood is all a-tingle
At the sound of blow on blow.
As I count each single shingle
On my bosky bungalow."

Burgess Johnson, "Bungal-Ode,"
Good Housekeeping, *February 1909*

The California bungalow—with its low profile, double gabled roofs, woodsy colors, and native boulders—was the original prototype (above). ■ In Seattle bungalows rose higher to capture water views but retained simplified Craftsman features such as exaggerated timberwork (opposite, top left). ■ Twin Cities builders preferred front-facing gables and moved the special effects indoors (top right). ■ Chicago developed a style of its own: narrow, built of brick, and featuring windows to soak up sun (bottom left). ■ Rail lines around Washington, D.C., made it easy to deliver mail-order houses such as the "Avalon" from Sears, advertised as being "from California" (bottom right).

n its 1908 bungalow planbook, the Radford Architectural Company of Chicago announced that the bungalow "is the result of the effort to bring about harmony between the house and its surroundings, to get as close as possible to nature." A natural house just large enough for an average family or a couple, built of natural materials and set in a garden—this was the essence of the bungalow's design.

Horizontal features tie it to nature, which inspired its muted tones of brown, tan, buff, red, and green recalling forest, desert, and prairie. Natural materials from wood clapboarding and shingles to native stone make a bungalow appear to have simply grown up in place like a well-nourished tree. Walls fade away, overshadowed by low roofs that sweep downward as a symbol of shelter. Only dormers announce that the ground-hugging house might have another story upstairs. Ornament is built in, gained naturally from color or honestly from exposed structural elements such as rafters and braces. Pleasing balance rather than strict symmetry is achieved. The landscaping and the porch embrace the outdoors, and generous windows bring nature indoors—their casements reaching outward to capture the breeze.

Covering all is the bungalow roof. The gable-front bungalow, recalling a Greek temple, was the most economical; a window in the upper story, which perhaps is shingled for contrast, brings light into the attic. A side-facing gabled roof, known as a shed roof, presents a broad expanse to the street; its central dormer or dormers are variously shedlike to match or gabled. Offset double gables are the hallmark of the California bungalow, while clipped gables, called jerkinhead gables, were adopted as Chicago's roof of choice to stress the horizontal line of the prairie. Hipped-roofed bungalows hearken back to the pyramidal thatched Indian *bengalas*. Recalling Japanese or Swiss features, gables that simulate the thrill of flight usually signify a larger and more complex house.

Surrounding the house and often a detached matching garage was a paradise of one's own making. Naturalized plantings of trees, shrubs, and flowers conveyed a cottage look, and vines united the house directly with the earth. A garden was required, said Gustav Stickley, "because in practically all of us is a deep, distinctive longing to possess a little corner of that green Eden from which our modern and materialistic ways of living have made us exiles."

Porches: Outdoor Living Rooms

What would a bungalow be without its porch? A cottage perhaps, but certainly not a bungalow. A veranda—an outdoor living room—has been a defining element of the bungalow since its origins in colonial India. "It was a sign of European 'adjustment' to the climate," explains Anthony D. King in *The Bungalow*, "a feature made necessary by the social as well as spatial separation of one dwelling from another and, as a space to spend one's spare time, it was a symbol of economic and political status."

In those earliest bungalows, a pyramid of thatch cascaded almost to the ground to shelter a shady, breezy portico beneath. After bungalows reached America's shores, most of their porches took one of two basic forms, both integrated into the body of the house: either tucked under a swooping side-facing gabled roof or sheltered underneath a front-facing gable that projects forward expressly to hold it. In contrast to the semipublic front porch, sleeping porches might be relegated to the house's private back side to capture the refreshing night air.

Serving as entrance as well as outdoor room and social center, the porch adds considerable architectural interest to the facade. Its skirt and piers, dressed in rustic materials ranging from stone to brick and concrete, underscore the bungalow's relationship to the earth. Half columns of wood or concrete, perhaps battered (flared) as a sign of strength, typically hold the roof. Railings toe the horizontal line. All expand the house's palette of shapes, textures, and colors.

Porches and attached vine-covered pergolas that seemed natural in California's climate required adjustments as bungalows moved into colder territory. Twin Cities residents enclosed their porches so they could use them in three or four seasons, and the Chicago bungalow further reduced the porch to just a covered entrance adjacent to a bright enclosed sunroom. "I'll tell you why we have small porches or stoops here. February," comments Bonita Mall of the Chicago Architecture Foundation. Open porches reappeared in more temperate Washington, D.C.

"With a few light tables, a book rack or two, and plenty of hammocks," suggested Gustav Stickley in *Craftsman Homes* (1909), "the veranda has all the sense of peace and permanency that should belong to a living room, whether indoors or out, that is habitually used by the family."

"Our little love nest
Beside a stream
Where red, red roses grow
Our bungalow
Of dreams."

Joe Verges, Tommie Malie, and Charles Newman, "A Bungalow of Dreams," 1927

Americans had been predisposed toward porches for a century when bungalows arrived. These outdoor rooms take an informal approach in the Rosemont neighborhood of Alexandria, Virginia (above), but are more rock solid in Pasadena's Bungalow Heaven (opposite, top left). ▪ Minneapolitans generally enclose theirs for cold-weather use (top right). ▪ The Seattle area's abundant cedar trees and glacial stones are ideal materials for rustic porches (bottom left). ▪ Chicago likes just enough cover to keep out the elements (bottom right).

*"A portrait on a wall
And friends will come to call. . . .
In a bungalow
For two."*

Dorothy Evans and Oz Hill,
"A Bungalow for Two," ca. 1950s

As a 1925 bungalow on Chicago's North Side illustrates, hallways were usually restricted to the bedroom and bathroom area (opposite, top). ▪ Bungalows such as one in Minneapolis replaced doors between living and dining areas with useful built-ins that subtly divided the space without doors (bottom). ▪ Henry L. Wilson, a Los Angeles architect who called himself the "Bungalow Man," offered scores of choices in his catalogues (below). Except for the luxury of a fireplace inglenook, two-bedroom layouts like this were built nationwide.

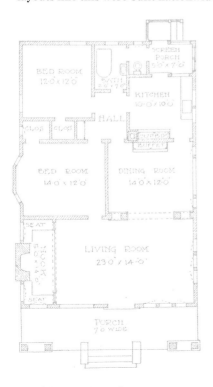

Inside: The Open Lifestyle

At the dawn of the twentieth century Frank Lloyd Wright was not alone in complaining that rooms had become little more than a series of constraining boxes. He promised to break down those walls, but the first to benefit in any number from this push to open up living spaces were bungalow owners. Builders across the country heeded both society's gravitation toward more relaxed lifestyles and reformers' pleas for more light and air in every room.

The front door of a typical bungalow opens directly into the living room, which replaced the unused parlor of the Victorian age. For Gustav Stickley, it was the most important room, "where the family life centers and from which radiates that indefinable home influence that shapes at last the character of the nation and the age." Within sight is the dining room, usually the bungalow's most formal space. "Equally symbolic," explained Stickley, "is our purpose in making the dining room either almost or wholly a part of the living room, for to us it is a constant expression of the fine spirit of hospitality to have the dining room, in a way, open to all comers." With its bosky wood features, from a built-in sideboard and paneling to box beams above, the dining room can nonetheless be "threateningly masculine," suggests Robert Winter.

In contrast, the kitchen was given over to the woman of the house. It was the bungalow's most modern space, touted as a factory or, by Wright, slightly more pleasingly as a laboratory. Cabinets replaced the pantry of old, and the arrangement of appliances and work spaces was honed to save all unnecessary steps. Bathrooms were similarly functional and, most important, looked sanitary. The standard combination of white bathtub, sink, and toilet was distinguished mainly by the pattern of the white tile around and below them. Bedrooms were also light in color, a restful contrast with the earthy browns, reds, greens, and golds used in the public rooms. At the back, a narrow stairway led to the attic, where as a family grew it usually added another two bedrooms and a bathroom.

For Stickley, houses like these "are based on the big fundamental principles of honesty, simplicity and usefulness,—the kind of houses that children will rejoice all their lives to remember as 'home'...."

Fireplaces: The Call of the Wild

As an architectural device, the fireplace transcends mere requirements for domestic warmth. The hearth has symbolized home and family togetherness since fires were built in caves—a fact that did not escape bungalow builders. Even though modern heating systems were becoming more accessible and affordable by the turn of the twentieth century, the open hearth with a roaring fire remained a potent symbol for the Arts and Crafts movement.

Both the chimney outside and the fireplace inside anchor a bungalow to the earth through the use of rough and rustic materials that set a house's color palette: ruddy brick, boulders laid as they were found in nature, dressed limestone, tile forged in high heat. Brick fireplaces, the bungalow workhorse, are seen coast to coast. In the West tile and large boulders were popular; stone sometimes came east in the form of river-rock facings. Chicago, where wire-cut brick predominates, is also known for its fake fireplaces—more symbol over substance.

Although the ideal was a fireplace rising from the floor to touch the ceiling—earth to sky—most bungalow hearths stop at a prominent mantel of quartersawn oak, fir, or cast concrete. Brick, almost always originally unpainted, may be corbelled to achieve integral decoration; mantels are sometimes bracketed to mirror exterior features. Openings tend to be rectangular, but occasional semicircular designs vividly recall the fire on the wall of the cave. Stickley liked a reflective copper hood, a luxury in a bungalow, as were inglenooks set apart in their own cavelike niche. As with other bungalow components, fireplaces and mantels could be ordered from a catalogue. In the 1920s Henry L. Wilson in Los Angeles, for example, pictured handsome cast-stone models with fanciful openings.

For Gustav Stickley, the fireplace was the center of the living room, the family's gathering place, and the space was to be planned around it. For Frank Lloyd Wright, a fireplace, as he said in 1896, was "the heart of the whole and of the building itself." For Henry H. Saylor, writing in his 1911 pattern book, *Bungalows: Their Design, Construction and Furnishings,* "a bungalow without a fireplace" was like "a garden without flowers." For bungalow owners fearful of changes in traditional family life, a wisp of smoke spiraling out of the chimney implied simply that all was right inside.

"In the quaint inglenook, with my pipe and my book,
I sit by the firelight's glow,
With Phyllis so fair, with the light on her hair,
In our own little Bungalow."

Stillwell and Company,
"There's a Little Side Street,"
Los Angeles, 1912

Californians were partial to tile fireplaces. In this Spanish bungalow in Pasadena, tile is used just to accent the plastered overmantel (above). The niche recalls old mission architecture.
■ A rustic brick fireplace is the focal point of this 1922 bungalow living room in Minneapolis (opposite). Built-in cabinets on either side carry the line of the oak mantel along the entire wall. On top is pottery by McCoy and Brush-McCoy.

Built-ins: Artistic Efficiency

The servants were gone, the space was smaller, but the emphasis on domestic efficiency had never been greater. Arts and Crafts enthusiasts and modern-home proselytizers alike proposed an "artistic" solution for all those possessions Americans were collecting: built-in furnishings and features. At once these helped eliminate the unnecessary, integrated interior ornament as an expression of honesty, unified a home's design, and freed up space in the center of rooms. Even Frank Lloyd Wright liked built-ins because they removed one more way in which homeowners might interfere with his architectural vision.

"Fittings for a bungalow should be as condensed as the equipment of a yacht," suggested Clarence E. Schermerhorn in William P. Comstock's *Bungalows, Camps and Mountain Houses* (1915). There were more possibilities than would fit any yacht: room dividers, bookcases, cabinets with art glass doors, fireside benches and inglenooks, window seats, radiator enclosures, buffets, wainscoting, plate rails, kitchen cupboards, a windowed breakfast nook, a folding kitchen table and ironing board, bedroom and linen closets, disappearing beds, medicine cabinets, a niche for the telephone. In architect-designed bungalows built-ins might be custom made, but for builders' bungalows, fixtures—even the breakfast nook, perhaps promoted as a "breakfastette"—could be ordered by number from national catalogues or local millwork suppliers. As a result, built-ins by and large remained free of significant regional variation, except for local wood preferences. Quartersawn oak, a universal choice, was supplemented by Douglas fir on the West Coast.

Wood set the tone from the floor—usually oak, with maple or pine reserved for the nonpublic spaces—to the ceiling. There ornamental box beams, made to appear structural, also came prefabricated from millwork catalogues. Stock wainscoting extending to a chair or plate rail, either paneled or filled in with burlap or canvas, made even small dining rooms seem luxurious. Plainer bead board lined kitchen and bathroom walls. Crown molding and sometimes a header band of wood running along the window and door tops reinforced the horizontal line. While simplifying interiors, such touches put craftsmanship within reach of bungalow residents. Today, when a bungalow door opens, the first and best surprise—every bungalow's "wow!" factor—is likely to be these interior extensions of the architecture itself.

"This is the song of the bungalow,
With a buffet built in the wall
And a disappearing bed beneath
That won't disappear at all. . . ."

"Ballad of the Bungalow,"
Architect and Engineer, *1914*

Once pantries were no longer needed to store large supplies of food, efficient built-in cabinets took their place in the kitchen itself (above). ▪ With its bucolic art glass backdrop, a buffet in the historic Parsons House in Altadena, California, is a bit more elaborate than those in most bungalows (opposite, left). ▪ Built-ins, which supposedly kept dust at bay, were considered a healthful household improvement. For all-white sanitary bathrooms such as in Craig Anderson's Minneapolis bungalow, medicine cabinets were usually built in as well (right).

Furnishings: The Finishing Touch

Craftsman furniture fits a bungalow in suburban Washington, D.C. (opposite), as well as it does one in California. The settle and the ladder-back caned chair at left are from Gustav Stickley, while the far chair is by Lifetime. A tall Limbert desk stands between the windows; the tall side table is by Michigan. ▪ Navajo rugs, although popular nationwide after the railroads opened up travel to the Southwest, especially suit this Spanish bungalow in Glendale, California (above). The Morris chair was made by Hardin.

With all their built-ins, bungalows came almost fully furnished. But there was still room for a little more: Morris chairs for reading by the fire, a slatted settle, perhaps a rocker and a piano, a round dining table and sturdy chairs, lamps, beds and dressers, rugs, draperies, and the bric-a-brac that set Arts and Crafts theorists to sermonizing. Homeowners were admonished by the likes of Gustav Stickley: "Only such furniture as is absolutely necessary should be permitted . . . , and that should be simple in character and made to harmonize with the woodwork in color and finish," he wrote in *Craftsman Homes* (1909). "From first to last the room should be treated as a whole. Such furniture as is needed for constant use may be so placed that it leaves plenty of free space in the room and when once placed it should be left alone."

What went best with the pared-down, masculine built-ins was furniture that followed suit—the Mission and Craftsman lines offered to buyers in every U.S. city by the Stickley brothers, the Roycrofters, Limbert, Lifetime, Sears, and scores of similar sources. Gone were the carved and curving lines of Victorian furnishings, and in their place came straightforward essays in woodworking complete with pegged joints. The natural grain of sturdy oak was decoration enough, leavened by a willow piece or two. Simple became beautiful, especially in the West, where rugged Mission furniture suited the bungalow's status as a retreat. "The foursquare furniture . . . obviously fit with the right angles of the interior design," notes Robert Winter.

From West to East, North to South, bungalows built during the heyday of the Arts and Crafts movement hewed to a similar line. Hammered-copper lamps in matte finishes with mica shades filtered light to a soft glow complementing the dark wood. Handmade Navajo rugs echoed the rectilinear furniture, while oriental rugs added an exotic counterpoint. Paneled curtains in coarse weaves, an embroidered nature motif lining the edge, filtered light and controlled air circulation, their ivory tones conveying sunlight. Plein-air paintings, quickly composed outdoors, brought nature inside. Indian pottery, weavings, and other handicrafts testified to America's own native artistry. "Everything," concluded Stickley, "should fall into place as if it had grown there before the room is pronounced complete."

BUNGALOWLAND

California bungalow. These two words have conjured up sweet dreams of a cozy home in paradise ever since the term was first used in 1905. "A bit of heaven, Beside a stream, I know you'll love it so, Our bungalow of dreams," pined the popular song "A Bungalow of Dreams" (1927). This "bungalonging" for a secluded little love nest began in the southern part of the Golden State, the warmer half, and floated over the San Gabriel Mountains to enthrall the rest of the country. So many bungalows were built in the Los Angeles area in the early twentieth century that a clever developer should have been inspired by the famous Hollywoodland sign to erect one announcing that this was actually Bungalowland.

Why Los Angeles? Founded in 1781 by Spanish settlers who named it El Pueblo de la Reina de los Angeles (Queen of the Angels), the cow town prospered on northern gold after the rush of 1849. A year later it was incorporated and then proceeded to turn itself into a land of fruit and honey, sending its local produce eastward and beckoning sun seekers westward, thanks to rail service that arrived beginning in 1876. From 50,000 in 1890, the population doubled to 100,000 by 1900, surging again between 1904 and 1906 and hitting one million by 1920, two million by 1930. Oil and water mixed in Los Angeles to help fuel this boom. William Mulholland's decade-long dream of filling city faucets with Owens Valley water (remember *Chinatown)* came true in 1913, and then in 1914 the opening of the San Pedro Harbor made Los Angeles the busiest West Coast port. No less important was celluloid, which the film industry shot by the mile given the assurance of almost daily sunshine in its new western home.

Bungalows soon became about as famous an export as Hollywood movies. Property could be had for a song, and in this temperate land of outdoor living, construction did not have to be strong enough to hold snow and ice at bay. Easier to build meant easier to pay for, especially for the retirees and young people who flocked to California to rent or

California perfected economical living with its numerous bungalow courts, a style that eventually transformed itself into roadside motels. Sherman J. McQueen designed and built the bucolic Harding Court in Monrovia about 1923, naming it for the president who died that year.

buy. Inventive architects rushed to California to exploit its new architectural frontiers. Real estate promoters touted their suburban developments, drawing newcomers to the city as well as to Santa Monica and Sierra Madre, Hollywood and Glendale, Pasadena and Altadena. Although automobiles eventually became Angelenos' favorite mode of transportation, Pacific Electric's Big Red trolleys moved "bungalowners" between home and office at the time these cities began to grow, adding to their attraction as good places to live. By 1930 ninety-four percent of all Los Angeles residences were single-family homes, an unprecedented number pumped up by the popularity of bungalows.

The bungalow and California were a match made almost literally in heaven. With land cheap and an expensive full basement unnecessary, large lots fifty feet wide opened the way for carefree one-story houses stretched out in league with the ground. Broad gabled roofs with deep overhangs provided needed shade, while verandas, sleeping porches, pergolas, and bands of windows annexed the outdoors. Rooms typically spread out on one floor, a boon to older residents. Materials native to the West, from redwood and Douglas fir to boulders plucked from dry riverbeds, fit the Arts and Crafts ideals of honesty and respect for nature. Shingles, clapboards, and complex timberwork all were combined for a vigorous profile, yet bungalows blended quietly into their surroundings with a color palette drawn from the desert and the forest.

Elements of Japanese temples and Swiss chalets can be found in California bungalows, but generally they followed the principles for Craftsman houses set out by Gustav Stickley and other Arts and Crafts proponents. As a result, the terms *Craftsman bungalow* and *California bungalow* often call to mind the same image of a low, woody retreat with front-facing gables set in a garden. Nothing epitomizes the style like California's "aeroplane" bungalows, their wings—outstretched beneath a dormered cabin—seemingly fashioned for flight.

Hardly anyone in the area could escape the bungalow drumbeat in the twentieth century's first two decades. Home magazines, Stickley's

Postcards trumpeted the California bungalow across the land (bottom left). This one shows the fittingly named "Hollywood" model from Sears. The Weaver House of 1911 in Santa Monica, with its mortise-and-tenon redwood posts, has a similar Craftsman ruggedness (bottom right).

The new driveway of this Craftsman bungalow in Pasadena's Bungalow Heaven proved a safe place to ride a tricycle. River rock, shingles, and assertive timberwork identify this as a prototypical California bungalow.

Craftsman, architecture journals, even the *Los Angeles Times* heralded this new way of living. The city had its own "Bungalow Man," Henry L. Wilson, an architect who published *Bungalow Magazine* here in 1909–10. Through catalogues he also offered full plans and specifications for $10 or, for custom designs, $5 a room. Many other entrepreneurs provided similar choices through their own bungalow planbooks. For those too impatient to wait three or six months, there were "ready-cut" bungalows—prefabricated homes offered locally by companies such as the California Ready-Cut Bungalow Company and Pacific Ready-Cut, which claimed to have built forty thousand bungalows. National mail-order companies such as Sears and Aladdin teased with offerings tagged the "Hollywood" and the "Pasadena."

Los Angeles was fortunate to have architects who took up the challenge of designing small homes for small pocketbooks. Some moonlighted to produce the anonymous designs featured in the builders' catalogues. Others, like the firm of Arthur S. (1878–1972) and Alfred Heineman (1882–1974), did both, leaving their imprint on some of the Southland's most charming and detailed bungalows. Sylvanus B. Marston (1883–1946), one of Pasadena's preeminent architects, designed freestanding bungalows as well as the Saint Francis Bungalow Court (1909). The Heinemans contributed the larger Bowen Court (1910), still in existence in Pasadena. The city's most noted architectural team remains that of the eminent Charles Sumner Greene (1868–1957) and his brother, Henry Mather Greene (1870–1954), whose legacy includes a refined group of "ultimate bungalows."

Even as Los Angeles developers by 1930 were opting to squeeze more people into apartments rather than let them luxuriate on single-family lots, word of California's great bungalow experiment had traveled eastward and taken hold. "The bungalow contributed to the privacy considered sacred by the middle class," observes Robert Winter in *The California Bungalow.* "The feeling of independence it gave, even on a tiny plot of land, is part of the freedom which even today one senses in southern California."

Pacific Overture

Our bungalow story begins in sight of the Pacific Ocean, high up on the crest of Santa Monica Canyon in what is considered Santa Monica's most spectacular location. This is where the eastern hotelier Henry Weaver alighted after he came west to retire peacefully in a state of nature. Completed in 1911, his rustic bungalow was designed by the firm that became Meyer and Holler, architects of the Hollywood fantasy Graumann's Chinese Theater (1927). Craftsman theatricality prevails here as well.

Wood gets star billing, from mortise-and-tenon redwood outside to Tabasco-colored mahogany paneling in the living room and wainscoting in the dining room fashioned of more traditional quartersawn oak. But all did not remain in pristine condition over the years. The cedar shingles were painted repeatedly and then sandblasted, the living room's oak floors were stained black, the iron-spotted brick fireplace sported a coat of white paint, and the paneling had started to crack.

The restoration architect Martin Weill helped new owners set things right beginning in 1985. The roof was replaced, rotting beams were replaced or restored, copper gutters were fabricated to match the originals, and a landscape of native plants was installed. Interior woodwork was refinished, in the process revealing oak panels in different grains resembling the coats of four different animals. Plaster walls disclosed original stenciling. From the downstairs to the old billiard room in the attic, everything including window sills, leaded-glass doors, bathrooms, and wall colors were uncovered and restored.

Yet more work was required to correct damage from the 1994 Northridge earthquake. The recipient of numerous restoration awards, Weaver's retirement bungalow is now listed in the National Register of Historic Places and is a state and local landmark as well. Says the California bungalow expert Robert Winter, with typical understatement, "This was not a commoner's bungalow."

Board-and-batten panels of quartersawn oak in the dining room rise to a bracketed plate rail (above). ▪ The stepped redwood corbels highlighting the low gabled roof and the mortise-and-tenon posts echo details of the "ultimate bungalows" that Greene and Greene were designing in Pasadena (opposite, top left and right). ▪ A Moorish arcade of windows in the living room is framed in reddish mahogany matching the wainscoting (bottom left). ▪ Above an unusual elliptical opening in the fireplace, exaggerated brackets support the prominent mahogany mantel (bottom right).

Low-Flying Object

As the only airplane bungalow in Santa Monica, Lori Nafshun and Mike Bone's 1912 house is an example of what Henry L. Wilson, Los Angeles's "Bungalow Man," liked to say "looks like more." Low wings dip down from the cockpit, beneath a rippling contrail of gabled roofs. It seems ready for takeoff—just like the early planes launched by the Wright Brothers beginning in 1903—and the style did just that, its asymmetrical look symbolizing the California bungalow's sense of freedom. Heavy redwood bargeboards, which surround a pierced gable vent at center, counteract any feeling of weightlessness.

"The house spoke to us," say the owners, who purchased the bungalow in the North of Montana area in 1992. "We knew little about the Arts and Crafts movement at the time. Now we're bungalow junkies." The original owner had started several cigarette fires, evidence of which can still be seen in burned hardwood floors. An interim owner restored the house and added a master suite at the back. The bungalow survived the 1994 Northridge earthquake, needing just chimney work, although other bungalows on the street were damaged beyond repair.

The 3,000-square-foot, three-bedroom house, now a designated Santa Monica landmark, features an array of built-ins from an inglenook to bookcases, a buffet, pocket doors, and disappearing beds. The family's favorite place is the sleeping loft tucked into the uppermost gable, which is shingled on the outside. It is surrounded by windows and, says Nafshun, "probably had an ocean view at one time, before the trees grew." Earth, air, fire, and water—the ground-hugging bungalow has seen it all.

Beyond the living room colonnade, French doors lead to a sunroom (below). The house's woodwork was painted by a previous owner.

Wide overhangs brush the complex layers of roofs with shade and shadow (opposite, top). Variegated redwood siding emphasizes the bungalow's horizontality, as does the low shed roof shielding the wraparound porch. Typical western stickwork, seen in the exposed rafter tails and double purlins, adds to the house's rustic appearance. ▪ Leaded glass in a diamond pattern fills the cabinet doors above the dining room's built-in buffet (bottom). Board-and-batten paneling covers the far wall, whose opening reveals the box-beam ceiling.

A four-foot-wide front door opens directly into the living room from the porch (above). Redwood siding blends the 2,500-square-foot bungalow into its setting. ▪ "The redwood ceiling in the living room appears to be the underside of the roof sheathing," says Tim Andersen, the restoration architect, "but it is not" (opposite). Instead he used redwood shiplap with "dummy rafters" that align with the true rafters. ▪ The house caught the Whalens' eye because it reminded them of the Ahwahnee Hotel (1927) in Yosemite. Sleeping porches at the back recall tree houses (below).

Arroyo Seco

Pasadena, located to the northeast of Los Angeles, was founded in 1874 by orange growers and became a resort town at the turn of the twentieth century. Along the arroyo near its western edge one can find poignant reminders of what California was like long ago when bungalows became all the rage. In this environment of fragrant eucalyptus trees, the more rustic a house is, the better it blends in.

Connie and Michael Whalen bought such a house in 1987, a redwood bungalow built in 1910 but moved a few blocks away eight years later. Local tradition calls it the work of Louis B. Easton (1864–1921), although this claim remains undocumented. Easton was a manual training instructor who began to design bungalows in Pasadena after moving west. He was the brother-in-law of Elbert G. Hubbard, founder of the Roycroft Colony in East Aurora, New York.

After the bungalow was moved in 1918, the prolific local architect Sylvanus Marston made additions to it, probably including the kitchen and the sunroom. By the time Tim Andersen began working with the Whalens on a restoration plan, original features had been removed and the floor plan was incoherent. The living room was, in Andersen's words, "a pink shoebox." Only the dining room was intact.

The family moved out to make way for restoration of the dining room, construction of a larger kitchen, renovation of the two bedrooms and bathrooms, addition of a stairway to the below-grade basement, and reconstruction of a deck. The biggest changes took place in the living room, which gained both width and dramatic height plus a missing fireplace. The architect also installed a large skylight in the hall to balance the light in the living room and the second bedroom while it floods the basement with light. "Because of the roof's low pitch, the skylight is not visible from anywhere outside," says Andersen, who specializes in restoring bungalows and other historic buildings in Pasadena and Seattle.

A final project was to rebuild the roof with its original integral gutters, wrapping it in a flexible roofing material that reminds Connie Whalen of Greene and Greene's Gamble House. "Bungalows that have lost their gutters and rafter tails through reroofing look flimsy—vaguely like postwar ranch houses," says Andersen. "This detail, perhaps more than any other, restores the exterior character of a Craftsman house."

No trace of the original fireplace existed, so Tim Andersen designed a new one to match the arroyo boulders used on the chimney (left). He added flanking clerestory windows to bring in light from above as well as to allow a view of the chimney from inside the house. ▪ Redwood is used throughout the interior, including for a board-and-batten window seat in the living room nestled beneath broad bands of windows (opposite). The family's Arts and Crafts furnishings are originals.

The stucco porch segues easily into a wooden pergola along the 1919 bungalow's right side, where the owners removed an added concrete screen (opposite, top). A garage at back mimics the house's clipped gables. ▪ Above the new built-in benches, double casement windows flank the lead-spotted brick fireplace (bottom left). Crown molding delineates both living and dining rooms. "We are rewarded every time we sit in these rooms," the Hitchcocks admit. ▪ Cabinets in the kitchen remain as they were in the Wingards' occupancy. Features include wainscoting made to resemble tile and an original California cooler (bottom right). The latter is a slatted vertical compartment for perishables such as fruits and vegetables that draws cool air from the basement or crawl space and vents in the ceiling or the wall.

All in the Family

Jacob and Lizzie Wingard were not about to let their son and daughter-in-law, Arthur and Mary Wingard, get ahead of them in the bungalow competition. The younger couple already owned a bungalow in what is now Pasadena's Bungalow Heaven when the elder Wingards came to visit in 1918, renting a bungalow a few doors away. Within a year the local contractor William Paget had designed the parents a three-bedroom, one-bathroom bungalow of their own at a cost of $3,835, one of at least two he put up in the area.

The neat one-story, 1,400-square-foot house sided in Douglas fir shows off a pair of offset jerkinhead gables, their tips clipped to preserve the horizontal line sought by all self-respecting bungalows. That sense of following the land is strengthened by bands of slatted vents beneath each gable and two sets of triple windows, which include casements paired with a fixed pane. A wide door lightened by a large glass oval leads into the living room, where new owners have done considerable work.

"When we purchased the house in 1999, all the woodwork in the front rooms was covered in beige paint and the walls with vinyl wallpaper," explain Kristin and David Hitchcock. "We stripped all the paint ourselves with a heat gun and chemicals—during a hot summer." They also replaced built-in benches on either side of the fireplace, the only evidence of which was "the shadow of the curve on the sides of the fireplace." Glass doors missing on the built-in dining room cabinets have also been restored.

The Hitchcocks have grown attached to Bungalow Heaven, Pasadena's first historic district. The area now encompassing about eight hundred homes was annexed by the city in 1906, at the beginning of the bungalow boom, and Craftsman examples soon filled its streets. In response to development threats, the district was created in 1989 (and named by the preservationist John Merritt). "Talking about our homes connects all of us in a way that is rare these days," notes Kristin. "Their front porches and fairly short front yards seem to encourage us to connect with one another." Now *Sunset* magazine has called Pasadena the "Best Neighborhood in the West."

What the Doctor Ordered

John C. Austin (1870–1963), one of southern California's leading architects, is known more for designing public buildings such as the Griffith Park Observatory, Los Angeles City Hall, Shrine Auditorium, hotels, schools, hospitals, office buildings, and churches. But he lived in Pasadena, where he took an active role in civic life, so when Robert Sutton, a physician, and his wife, Orpha, asked him to design a house in Bungalow Heaven in 1915, Austin agreed. From the street it is obvious that this is not a standard-issue, planbook bungalow. Lee Root, who built four houses in Bungalow Heaven, supervised the construction.

The architect took typical bungalow features—double gables, jerkinhead roofs, a broad front porch—and scrambled them up a bit just for fun. The front gable, which flares ever so slightly, is turned diagonally for maximum impact. Exaggerated rafter tails and purlin beams come forward around the slotted vent as if in welcome. Subtle soldier courses catch the light on the brick columns holding the wraparound porch. After new owners James and Andrea Galloway purchased the 1,550-square-foot, three-bedroom house in 1977, they removed aluminum siding to discover intricate shingles underneath.

Inside, the original Douglas fir woodwork, light fixtures, and hardware fared better, remaining unchanged through the years. Although the living room is comparatively small, it gains visual space from the adjacent open study. A side porch can easily be seen through the dining room's French doors. Built-ins add to the efficiency: a mirrored sideboard, wainscoting, and a plate rail in the dining room; a desk and bookcases in the study; a china cabinet in the kitchen.

A tiled fireplace dominates the living room. Above it is an impressive bracketed mantel of Douglas fir and an overmantel displaying plain and decorative tiles with a leaf motif that Jim hopes is not ivy. "As we would love to ban ivy from Bungalow Heaven," he says, "I refuse to believe it to be that dreaded plant." Adds Jim, who is active in the Bungalow Heaven Neighborhood Association, "We have a saying in Bungalow Heaven: 'You come for the architecture, you stay for the neighborhood.'"

Broad steps lead up to the twelve-light oak door (above). The brick columns were rebuilt following earthquake damage. An unfinished attic is above. ▪ Jim Galloway's grandmother traded a broken-down Model T truck in the early 1900s for the Seth Thomas mantel clock (opposite). "It still keeps perfect time," he says.

Log Heaven

I n the summer of 1912 three speculative houses were built side by side in what is now Bungalow Heaven, part of a group of eight constructed on one street by City Builders Investment Company. All were designed by Norman F. Marsh (1871–1955), whose large Los Angeles firm had laid out the canal-filled town of Venice in 1904. Like other noted area architects who dabbled in bungalows, he had local ties, including a home in South Pasadena.

Frank Forbes, the first owner of this imaginative bungalow—built for a bargain $2,400—rented it out until deciding to sell in 1917. The new owners were Charles and Isabelle Johnston, who stayed put for fifty-five years, raising their two daughters here. When the younger child, Mary Helen, was seven years old, the city bus made a special stop in front of the bungalow to pick her up on her way to violin lessons, which paid off after she was later selected to play in the Pasadena Symphony. During World War II she brought her own son, Keith, back here while her husband, Glen Dawson, was in the army. Later the couple operated Dawson's Bookshop in Los Angeles.

Owned by one family for such a long time, the 1,400-square-foot house escaped many of the insensitive changes that can happen with transient residents. The interior woodwork, which is Douglas fir stained to look like more expensive hardwood, retains its original finish, as do the oak floors. Crown molding, box beams, wainscoting, a built-in buffet, a colonnade separating living and dining rooms, and the original roller screens all would look familiar to the Johnstons. The house includes a front parlor or bedroom, two other bedrooms, a breakfast room, and an enclosed sun porch off the dining room.

The current owners since 1997, Doug and Keri Axel, have remodeled the kitchen, incorporating the former back porch and adding a banquette and linoleum flooring. "We recently became acquainted with the Johnstons, which has connected us to the house's past and made us feel privileged to be part of its future," say the Axels. "We cannot imagine living anywhere else."

With its low-pitched rolled roof and dramatic timberwork, the bungalow wears a subtle Japanese mien (opposite, top). Elongated shingles surround two expansive trios of front windows. ▪ Bold stucco pillars accented with brick anchor the porch (bottom left). The curved timbers on top are echoed in brackets supporting the dining room's plate rail. ▪ In the bungalow's living room a whimsical cast-concrete fireplace, a Marsh signature, brings the woods right indoors (bottom right). Built-in window seats are located on either side.

Hearth and Home

Even with double gables, the bungalow keeps a low profile (opposite, top). The pair of battered stucco piers add muscle to the facade. ▪ A lively shingle pattern above a stucco skirt and exposed rafter tails lend the bungalow a picturesque Swiss chalet appearance (bottom left). ▪ The fireplace's cavelike opening reinforces the primordial appeal of fire (bottom right). For those who prefer seating less rustic than the boulders, a built-in bench is nearby.

t was one thing for Frank Lloyd Wright or Arts and Crafts architects to build a house around the hearth in the cold Midwest, and another thing entirely for designers in sunny southern California to follow suit. But it did not escape bungalow builders that a fireplace would clinch the deal on coziness. And what better example to follow than that of Greene and Greene, who had discovered the architectural value of California's boulders as symbolic links to the land?

The rustic fireplace of this house in Pasadena's Bungalow Heaven, built in 1912 by the contractors Kieft and Hetherington for Claude E. Markey, a dentist, conveys the same compelling sense of hearth and home as the one in the Greene brothers' Camp House (1904) in Sierra Madre. Large river rocks slide down toward two impressive boulders forming the hearth and simultaneously providing a place to sit and warm one's toes after a vigorous hike in the great outdoors. To make it clear that this area is the center of the house, the built-in bookcase puts reading matter close at hand.

Like the bookcase, the house's other woodwork is Douglas fir with a dark stain: cabinets in a built-in colonnade, a buffet, plaster-and-batten wainscoting, a plate rail, box beams, crown molding, doors, and window surrounds. When James Crandall and Nancy Phillips found the house, the interior was completely white. "We learned that some of the woodwork under the paint was original, but much was not," explains Crandall, an artist. "We stripped and restained and removed some additions."

A twin down the street built by the same company served as a reference for reconstruction of the missing colonnade, built-in bookcases, and bench seat. For a 1980s addition that enlarged the house from 1,250 to 1,650 square feet, the owners went back to the teens so that its studio and third bedroom would be more in keeping with the bungalow's style. "Our guiding principle was to resist any temptation to mimic a detail of a higher-style house."

Builders' Best

With bungalow fever raging in Pasadena in 1910, it was not unusual for contractors and property developers to buy multiple lots and put up bungalows on each. One such contractor was John K. Johnsen, who built eleven houses between 1909 and 1912 in what is now Bungalow Heaven. The local real estate speculator Harvey H. Vincent was another. He owned eighteen lots on just two streets, North Michigan and North Chester, and built five houses on North Michigan between 1910 and 1917. Like bungalow developers across the country, he moved sequentially into different houses as they were built. But as their second of three houses in Pasadena, Vincent and his wife, Etta, in 1910 bought this tall Swiss chalet—a house owned by Johnsen—and did not move into one of Vincent's own speculative houses until two years later. By 1919 he had disappeared from city directories.

The design of this three-bedroom bungalow, built for $2,800, is unlike other Johnsen houses and at two stories high is unusual for the neighborhood. Occupying the first floor are living and dining rooms, the kitchen, a bathroom, and a downstairs bedroom, now a den, that projects into the yard under a gabled roof. Two bedrooms, a sunroom, and another bathroom are upstairs. To many the overscaled upper story, with stickwork embellishing its front gable, conjures up images of Switzerland. No one in southern California really needed a lookout above snow drifts, but the perpetual yearning for the picturesque prevailed.

Inside the 2,200-square-foot bungalow, owned since 1983 by Cindy and Tom Rice, all is cozy under vaulted ceilings. Douglas fir stained a dark color sets the tone right over the threshold, from door surrounds, box beams, and built-in bookcases to a pair of built-in buffets in the dining room. Yet it was the five-car garage in back that attracted Tom, an automotive machinist and auto buff. "He keeps the garage full at all times," says Cindy, although part is used as a workshop. Both grew up in Pasadena, she adds, "and both of our families lived in Bungalow Heaven at some time or another." In the 1920s her grandfather operated the first plumbing shop on wheels from his house three blocks away.

An earthy tone around the casement windows and on the recessed vent combines with the green-painted redwood shingles to evoke a leafy forest (opposite). The partially roofed pergola is supported by pairs of half columns atop sturdy stucco piers. Stickwork in a side gable repeats the design of the front dormer. ▪ Above the intricate iron-spotted brick fireplace in the living room hangs a plein-air–style painting by the Rices' neighbor James Crandall (below).

GOD GRANT ME
SERENITY TO ACCEPT THE
THINGS I CANNOT CHANGE
COURAGE TO CHANGE THOSE
THINGS I CAN AND WISDOM
TO KNOW THE DIFFERENCE

A built-in bench greets visitors in the entrance hall, a space atypical for a bungalow given that most opened directly into the living room. Here pocket doors lead left into the dining room or right into the living room. The floors are oak.

Carpenter's Holiday

The purchase of a new car in 1921 was noteworthy enough to make the pages of the *Pasadena Star-News.* "'Another Nash' Sold by Local Distributors to One of Busy Business Men of Pasadena," the paper reported on November 26. The busy businessman pictured in the story was Sherman Seeds, a contractor who arrived in Pasadena in 1905 to work as a carpenter. Within five years he was on his own, building several houses in Bungalow Heaven. He lived in one completed in 1913 until finishing this $4,500 bungalow in 1919, when he moved in with his wife, Mary Corinne.

"This house has been well loved for decades and is currently well loved by us," says Teresa Hartley, who has made her home here since 1995 with her husband, James Staub. They have a pared-down Craftsman with jerkinhead (clipped) gables on the front and side and few exposed structural elements; a broad front dormer above repeats the roof shape. A mixture of quartersawn oak and Douglas fir, never painted— oak floors downstairs and maple upstairs plus a wealth of original cabinetry—heats up the interior. More delicate molding than the usual Craftsman style encircles the plaster ceilings.

A den on the first floor probably started out as a maid's room (the kitchen door also boasts a maid's window). One of the three upstairs bedrooms that is now enclosed appears to have been a sleeping porch. The master bedroom provides a "living plein-air painting" of Mount Wilson. Both bathrooms are original.

About five families have lived in the house over the years, some of whom have returned to reminisce. One drops by regularly, says Hartley, adding, "A gentleman from Sweden who lived here in the 1940s remarked that the interior looks exactly like he remembers—only smaller. Houses seem to grow bigger in our memory." Another former resident ran her hands along the wood to find where she had carved her name as a child. "She pointed out the upside-down house that her brother carved on a door," Hartley noted. Yet, given that the builder left his name imprinted in concrete in the back yard, the house will probably always be known as the Seeds bungalow.

Identical shingles, flush trim, and totally square wood posts on cast-concrete piers add to the 2,140-square-foot bungalow's no-nonsense look (above, at left). Beneath the porch's hipped roof sits a mortise-and-tenon Douglas fir swing custom made by Sherman Seeds for the house. ▪ Separating the living and dining rooms is a divider with battered fir columns, which direct the eye toward a built-in sideboard that fills the dining room's entire far wall (opposite). The Steuben glass chandelier is a later addition.

Wainscoting was added to the breakfast room, whose high window opens onto a back porch that was originally screened (above). A corner cabinet is also built in here. ▪ Handsome fir cabinets line the kitchen, whose countertops are finished with sanitary white hexagonal tile (right). A drop-down table located in this room may have been used by the maid.

Civic Improvement

Cyril Bennett (1891–1957) was just twenty-three years old when he designed this tribute to stone and wood, one of his first commissions after he started his own architecture practice. The 1,650-square-foot bungalow, which cost $3,500, was among ten plans he produced in 1914 for the J. H. Woodworth and Son real estate firm, seven of which remain on one Pasadena block. Most of his training came from Sylvanus Marston, one of Pasadena's preeminent architects. By 1919 Bennett had designed three dozen houses in the city.

That he worked even briefly with Greene and Greene might be surmised from the architect's bold use of stone for the porch piers and chimney or simply from his mastery of the California idiom. As the owner notes, "The exterior is almost a textbook example of how to create horizontal lines." The light-colored beltcourse and header, the porch beam, and the porch railing all align the house closely to the ground, with only the pair of offset gables and the vertical thrust of the chimney adding a slight lift skyward.

The beltcourse motif continues indoors, where a header of dark-stained Douglas fir below the crown molding paints a simplified frieze around the living and dining rooms. The divider between them never had columns above its battered piers. At the back of the two-bedroom, one-bathroom house is a breakfast room whose French doors with side casement windows open it directly onto a pergola-covered porch. "It's a great example," says the owner, "of a spec house done with pride by developers who believed they were truly improving the area."

Pasadena had arroyo stone for the taking early in the twentieth century, and architects and builders put it to dramatic use (below). ▪ A beltcourse crisply divides the clapboards from the shingles around the bands of windows (opposite). A similar coping of brick tops the massive stone piers and chimney. Winged gables and rafter tails add counterbalance.

The owners bought the bungalow "to match our collection of Arts and Crafts furniture." A seven-foot-wide pressed-brick fireplace provides a warm backdrop for their L. & J. G. Stickley slant-arm Morris chair and an unsigned oak footstool (opposite). The library table is by Limbert. On the mantel are pieces from Fulper and Heintz Art Metal. ▪ A Gustav Stickley table and chairs match the simplicity of the dining room (above). Fulper pottery sits on the table and the sideboard, which has its original hardware and glass.

Flight of Fancy

Seemingly poised for liftoff, this airplane bungalow in Bungalow Heaven is nonetheless firmly tethered to the ground. Great heaps of arroyo stone were piled up to form a porch as protected as a stony cave. Its broad covering is mirrored by another low gabled roof set back over the pilot's cabin (actually two upstairs bedrooms). From its sense of freedom to its earthy textures and colors, the house captures the essence of the California bungalow. Its street once offered spectacular views across the San Gabriel Valley, taking in downtown Los Angeles and Catalina Island.

John A. Jergenson designed and constructed the bungalow in 1914 for $4,000, one of two he built in Pasadena. Throughout he used oak for the floors, Douglas fir for the woodwork, and plaster for the ceilings. The house's 1,950 square feet include a breakfast room, a laundry, four bedrooms, bathrooms upstairs and down, and an unfinished basement. An open sleeping porch at the back of the second floor was enclosed as a closet before Mike and Susan Lange arrived in 1986.

They have converted that porch into a bathroom, in addition to removing paint from the woodwork, restoring the dining room wainscoting, refinishing the oak floors in the dining and living room after removing their linoleum covering, restoring the plaster ceilings, and remodeling the kitchen. "We've done most of the nonconstruction renovation ourselves," they note, adding that the work became a family affair. Husband, wife, brother, and sister all got into the act, building furniture and doors, making curtains and pillows, and adding stenciling that all fall into place as naturally inside as the stones and wood outside.

Layers of front- and side-facing gables, stone and shingles, and solids and voids all combine to give this tall bungalow a vigorous exterior (left). Pocket casement windows open up three sides of the upper story. ▪ The owners have planted natural borders and gardens showcasing perennials, roses, and orchids (above). Earthquake damage to the chimney and porch has been repaired. ▪ Previous owners removed both the dining room's original wainscoting and a built-in sideboard (opposite). The Craftsman-inspired dining set, centered on one of the couple's oriental rugs, was made by the owner's brother, Charles Lange.

Alive with oak branches swaying in the art glass, the front door opens into the house's formal stair hall (opposite and above). Rounded timbers of carved Burmese teak set the tone for what unfolds. At left is a guest bedroom. ▪ Despite its three stories, capped by a belvedere, the Gamble House stretches out to hug the ground with low overhanging gables, cantilevered roofs, and exposed rafters that paint the shingled facade with welcome shade (right). ▪ In the living room inglenook, wood pauses for a moment to reveal an iridescent tile fireplace whose trailing vine design brings nature right into the hearth (overleaf).

Ultimate Bungalow

To find one of Pasadena's "ultimate bungalows" (a term coined by the Greene and Greene scholar Randell Makinson), a visitor must leave Bungalow Heaven for Westmoreland Place and the house designed in 1908 for David and Mary Gamble by Charles Sumner Greene and his brother, Henry Mather Greene. In truth not a bungalow in conception, size, craftsmanship, or cost, the Gamble House nonetheless shared with bungalows their Arts and Crafts sensibilities, benefited from the example of early Craftsman houses, and inspired bungalow builders in California and beyond.

Arriving in Pasadena in 1893, when the city was still young, the architects soon devised a unique design vocabulary that melded a number of languages: the open plans of Shingle-style houses in the East, the artistry of Asia, an Arts and Crafts affinity for simplicity and nature, a respect for craftsmanship, and an abundance of malleable native materials right on their doorstep. "The spell of Japan is on him," said the British historian C. R. Ashbee about Charles Greene, adding that "he feels the beauty and makes magic out of the horizontal line...." Greene and Greene houses—which came first, beginning in 1902—certainly had this in common with California bungalows.

The Gamble House, built as a retirement home for the son of a Procter and Gamble founder, is a complete work of art. From the front doorway with its iridescent glass crafted by Emil Lange to its incomparable teak joinery, tilework, lighting, hardware, and furnishings handcrafted in the workshop of Peter and John Hall, not a feature or a fixture was left to the owner's discretion. In sleeping porches, an expansive terrace, rock-filled walls, and the very wood that formed its timbers, the house embraced nature. Greene and Greene, said the American Institute of Architects in 1952, were "formulators of a new and native architecture ... recognized throughout the world, influencing the design of small as well as great houses."

A Moving Experience

The idea of the California bungalow moved quickly across the country, but in at least one case a quintessential California bungalow itself had to be moved. It happened in 1980, when the historic Parsons House—designed by the noted firm of Arthur and Alfred Heineman—was cut up into three sections, minus its granite porch and chimney, and trucked four miles from Pasadena to Altadena ("above Pasadena") to save it from demolition. After developers had eyed the 1910 bungalow's original site, the house was donated to Pasadena Heritage and sold for a dollar to Phil Elkins. He called in the architect Tim Andersen to help put the pieces back together in the new location, which had to be filled in and graded to match the original flat site.

Although the neighbors were at first distressed by the Frankenstein's monster that appeared on their doorstep that day, the three-bedroom house "has now become a neighborhood landmark where neighbors are always welcomed," say Mary Quirk and William Steinberg, the owners since 1984. "It's always thrilling to see visitors' faces as they first view the wonderful handcrafted woodwork in the living and dining rooms—just like our own first reactions." Among Pasadena's most skilled bungalow designers, the Heineman brothers' way with wood approached that of those other designing brothers from Pasadena, the Greenes.

"It took more than two years to complete the sizable job," explains Andersen. "We could have built a reproduction of the house for much less than what it cost to restore. Had we all been less enthusiastic and naive about the project, the house would probably not have been saved."

In 1997 the owners asked Andersen to design a guest house, which was added onto the garage and now steps gently down the hill. It shares a garden with the house without overshadowing the bungalow. Viewing the old house from the new guest house terrace at sunset, Quirk and Steinberg marvel that "the oak glows with a warmth similar to many of our beautiful golden sunsets." What the Heinemans could not have planned for in their original bungalow was the spectacular views of the San Gabriel Mountains the dining and breakfast rooms now offer—one serendipitous benefit of the relocation.

The exceptional woodwork runs to beamed oak ceilings and an unusual pediment over the inglenook that mimics the house's roofline (above). The bungalow originally cost $5,000. ▪ In his architecture Alfred Heineman paid special attention to ceilings. The oak colonnade in the dining room rises to a latticework divider, a perfect frame for the magnificent mirrored buffet (opposite). The pièce de résistance is the landscape scene above etched in Tiffany-style glass. The teak table is Danish.

Tucked into a niche one step up just inside the front door, the extraordinary inglenook is a bungalow-sized match for Greene and Greene's work, from its masterful quartersawn oak to the sinuous brown tile (left). ▪ New arroyo boulders define the 2,500-square-foot redwood-shingled house, which seems to emerge naturally from the earth (opposite, top left). Brick coping on the low walls mirrors the zigzagging of the low gabled roofs. ▪ The new guest house, based on southern California painters' studios, includes a living-dining room, bedroom, bathroom, courtyard, and terrace (top right). ▪ Entering the refined guest house, visitors usually exclaim: "I want to move in!" (bottom).

All-American Bungalow

"Bungalows were just too common where I grew up to warrant much special attention," says John Brinkmann, founder and publisher of *American Bungalow* magazine, who lived in a Williamsburg-style bungalow southeast of Los Angeles. The bug did not bite him until after he had purchased the locally revered Twycross house, a 1914 airplane bungalow in Sierra Madre, just northeast of Pasadena. This is the bungalow that inspired the magazine that has inspired countless people to join the modern bungalow boom. "If we weren't the spark that started it all," says Brinkmann, "we certainly have been part of the fuse."

For nearly three quarters of a century, Ruth Twycross remained in the shingled bungalow built for her and her husband, Converse, as newlyweds. In 1930 R. M. Finlayson of Monrovia added Spanish colonial features inside as part of an expansion to three bedrooms. Brinkmann bought the bungalow in 1987 to serve as his graphic design office, a facet of his life that has been overshadowed since the magazine's launch here in 1990. Today the staff has grown to about a dozen, with half working out of their historic quarters every day.

"Although the material rewards of working on *American Bungalow* were far less than those of my design business, the satisfaction of hearing that another threatened neighborhood has been saved is a deeper and far more gratifying form of payment," Brinkmann muses. "A return to the bungalow is under way, because it fulfills a need similar to the one that made it popular in the early twentieth century. The added fact that bungalows are now old and reminiscent of a quieter time will ensure their popularity for years to come," he prophesies. "On top of that, a sense of community often adds to bungalows' homey appeal. America's twenty-first-century frontiers are its bungalow neighborhoods." And for Brinkmann himself? "My dream is a rustic bungalow somewhere on a lake or a stream."

The stone piers and chimney, double front gables, and exposed rafter tails make the magazine's home a prototypical California bungalow (opposite, top). Removal of years of paint built up on the crosscut shingles proved a frustrating task. But, asks Editor Michelle Gringeri-Brown, "Isn't it nice to know that our American bungalow is just like yours? A place of comfort and great joy, while a never-ending source of projects and potential." ▪ Another project is to restore the original wraparound porch (bottom left). *American Bungalow* may eventually move some of its operations out of the house to help preserve it. ▪ Original kitchen fixtures and furnishings retain the bungalow's residential character (bottom right).

Hilltop Hacienda

Not only did California launch the bungalow movement, it also helped fuel a craze in the 1920s for Spanish colonial architecture. In the last years of the nineteenth century, designers seeking a style fitted to the West found inspiration in the state's historic Spanish missions. After the Panama-California Exposition was held in San Diego in 1915, the earlier pared-down Mission style became full-fledged paeans to the buildings of old Spain—from red tiled roofs over stucco walls to arched windows and elaborate ironwork.

This Spanish revival found its way, however simplified, to bungalows throughout the Los Angeles region and soon on across the country. In hilly Glendale, north of the city, the style's large arched windows proved ideal for capturing views of the San Gabriel and Verdugo Mountains. G. D. Turner, a carpenter-builder, erected this bungalow in 1927, wrapping it around a small patio that maximizes opportunities for outdoor living. Seventy years later a methodical collector of cowboy and Indian artifacts, pottery, and Arts and Crafts furniture made the house his museum.

Dennis Fosdick, a water polo coach, restored the tiled roof and then, as a preventive measure for his earthquake-prone aerie, had the house bolted to the foundation. Next came the fun part: finding niches for his Stickley, Limbert, Hardin, and J. M. Young furniture; his Weller, Rookwood, and Bauer pottery; his Navajo rugs and beadwork. He casually installed his cowboy saddle in a corner of the dining room, beneath an antique chandelier whose thunderbird and arrow motifs prompted a frieze around the room's coffered ceiling. Fosdick's interior designer, Karen Hovde, designed this and another frieze in the living room featuring stencilled arrows. In this completely western bungalow, cowboys and Indians are peacefully united.

The dining room's rainbow-colored, stencilled frieze was inspired by the light fixture, a lucky find (right). Beyond an oak table encircled by Gustav Stickley chairs and next to an Ulrich hutch is Fosdick's antique saddle. The braided lariat in the foreground has lassoed a settle by L. & J. G. Stickley.

Red tiled roofs atop pale stucco walls reflect the Spanish architectural revival of the 1920s (opposite, top). ▪ Arched windows are echoed indoors in arched openings between rooms (bottom left). ▪ With their bright colors recalling the sun-washed Mediterranean, Bauer dishes and Bakelite utensils are at home in the breakfast nook (bottom right). On the 1904 Gustav Stickley table is a period table runner.

THE EMERALD CITY

Seattle may be known as the Emerald City for its lush greenery, but another color lingers in the memory here: the burnished red of bungalows fashioned from Douglas fir trees that once anchored the hillsides above Puget Sound. And it was real gold, not figurative emeralds, that drove settlers into the country's northwestern reaches in the mid-nineteenth century. For those who stayed, as well as for those who returned richer or poorer from Alaska's gold fields, the community that developed in sight of the jagged Olympic Mountains to the west and the volcanic Cascades to the east proved to be a welcoming place to put down roots. Between 1909 and 1920, many of the recent arrivals did so in bungalows relying on native materials and framing picture-postcard views of snow-capped mountains and glassy lakes.

Seattle got its start in 1851, when a party led by Arthur Denny sailed up from Oregon to tame the wilderness on the shores of Elliott Bay. These pioneers named their settlement New York Alki (Chinook for "by and by") but soon decamped for more agreeable territory across the bay, where a new name, Seattle, honored a friendly leader of one of the Coast Salish tribes. Within two years Henry Yesler began skidding logs downhill to his famous steam-driven sawmill and Washington joined Oregon as a U.S. territory. Over time the railroads brought more settlers out from the East and the Midwest, but it was lumber that kept them here. Seattle boomed on a tide of harvested old-growth trees shipped out to ports near and far, adding shipbuilding and maritime trade to its list of economic mainstays that ran the gamut from lumber and railroads to gold and banking.

After an 1889 fire burned through Seattle's downtown, architects came west to help rebuild. By 1900 designers trained in England or Germany brought the city a new aesthetic, one grounded not in classical styles but instead in the Arts and Crafts movement and medieval revivals. With their emphasis on natural materials, particularly wood—which Seattle had in abundance—the resulting buildings fit the rugged

Jud Yoho's *Bungalow Magazine* featured this Ellsworth Storey design in Mount Baker on the cover of its March 1916 issue. Similar blends of California and Prairie features can be seen throughout the Northwest.

By 1921 Seattle neighborhoods had filled up with bungalows such as the one in the middle on Carleton Avenue South (right), which cut a modest profile compared to its Victorian cottage neighbor on the right.

Pacific Northwest landscape like another branch on a tall tree. The city even gained its own Arts and Crafts community near the eighteen-mile-long Lake Washington in 1908, when the Beaux Arts Society founded a village centered around a log bungalow.

Promoting the city as the "Gateway to the Orient," the Alaska-Yukon-Pacific Exposition of 1909 put Seattle firmly on the American map. A year later the city marked a population of 237,000 residents, a spurt of more than fivefold over the past two decades. A proponent of City Beautiful planning principles, it was also the "City Practical," as the historian Lawrence Kreisman suggests in *Made to Last: Historic Preservation in Seattle and King County*, enumerating "engineering feats on a scale seldom attempted in an American city": heroic regrading of its hills, infilling of shorelines, digging of shipping channels, creation of parks and parkways by designers such as the Olmsted Brothers. Ferries and, beginning in 1902, an interurban electric rail line and cable cars strung it all together.

Seattle's burgeoning middle class needed homes, and like their neighbors to the south in the heart of bungalowland, residents increasingly turned to bungalows. Inexpensive plans were everywhere: in builders' planbooks, in trade and popular periodicals such as *Bungalow Magazine* (published in Seattle from 1912 to 1918), and in newspapers. Even enterprising architects got into the business. As early as 1907 $25 would buy plans and specifications from Victor W. Voorhees, W. W. DeLong, or Elmer Ellsworth Green, whose *Practical Plan Book* in 1912 showed sixty choices. Most cost from $1,000 to $4,000 to build, and terms and lots were available starting at $100 to $150 down. For a larger outlay, a custom-designed bungalow might be had from the likes of Ellsworth Storey (1879–1960), a Chicago transplant who gained local renown for sensitive Arts and Crafts buildings with a Swiss lineage, work that helped forge a Northwest regional style. Andrew Willatsen (1876–1974) came out from Frank Lloyd Wright's studio in Oak Park, Illinois, bringing a bit of the Prairie style with him.

The spunkiest bungalow entrepreneur, Seattle's own bungalow man, was Jud Yoho (1882–1968). He arrived with the Yukon gold rush in 1897 and built bungalows under the imprimatur of the Craftsman

Bungalow Company from 1911 to 1917, all the while publishing *Bungalow Magazine.* Yoho used that forum to promote the company's bungalow plans, showcasing the best California had to offer alongside his own designs—adapted to Seattle's hilly topography and cooler climate—and those of his associate, Edward L. Merritt.

Seattle bungalows drew on the California model as well as the Pacific Northwest's own distinctive natural materials to craft a rough-hewn, homemade look. Some adopted details from Japan—inspired by the city's trade with Japan, its large Japanese community, and the popularity of the Japanese tea garden at the 1909 Yukon exposition—or from chalets that had long graced the folds of faraway mountains not unlike Seattle's own Mount Rainier and Mount Baker. Weather-resistant cedar siding and shingles (the world's largest shingle industry could be found in Ballard), river rocks, vine-covered trellises, fences, gardens, box-beam ceilings, and old-growth fir woodwork all reinforced the idea of the bungalow as a rustic retreat in paradise. Board-and-batten wainscoting, its Douglas fir crosscut like quartersawn oak to reveal the reddish grain, is a recurring feature, as are Western Stick Style attributes from decorative gables to dramatically bracketed overhangs. With many urban lots as narrow as twenty-five feet, paradise sometimes had to be shoehorned in, uphill and down.

The region's hills and water barriers shaped the development of Seattle and its environs, turning the area into distinct villages, many of them eventually annexed to the city. What all neighborhoods had in common were bungalows, from casual vacation retreats in West Seattle to architect-designed cabins tucked into the planned wilderness of Denny Blaine in the northeast, hugging Lake Washington. Queen Anne Hill to the northwest, Wallingford on Lake Union, and Ravenna-Roosevelt north of downtown; Montlake to the east; Leschi and Mount Baker to the south— all were settled around the time the bungalow became America's economical home of choice. In the July 1912 *Architectural Record*, Herbert Croly, its editor, suggested that Seattle was a "City of Great Architectural Promise" but called its residences "disappointing." The present owners of sought-after bungalows built around this time could not disagree more.

For a bungalow in picturesque Denny Blaine, Ellsworth Storey turned to Swiss chalets for inspiration (bottom left and right). Exterior and interior doors carry his signature diagonal muntins top and bottom.

Mount Rainier in View

Just as the Japanese reckon by Mount Fujiyama, Seattle residents use the glacier-wrapped Mount Rainier, the signature of the Cascade Range, as their compass point. Many of those who live on the steep hillsides of the Leschi neighborhood east of Pioneer Square can count on views of the state's highest mountain, but it was the Lake Washington shoreline that attracted Indian and later settlers. Views of both from an uphill corner lot proved irresistible to the owners when they first came upon this 1910 Craftsman bungalow.

"The house was in bad shape," they admit, but they liked its commanding presence, the welcoming porch, the spaciousness, the wood paneling, the built-ins. Working with Larry Johnson and Howard Miller of the Johnson Partnership and Laurie Taylor of Ivy Hill Interiors, they made relatively minor changes that produced a major impact. First came removal of inappropriate modifications to the porch and replacement of the roof. Sometime after 1936 a previous owner had installed colonial-style brick columns in place of the original piers and posts. The paired dormers, which had also been remodeled, were altered to lower the sills, which made way for window seats underneath and bookshelves to the side. All the woodwork was refinished or replaced. The kitchen and the upstairs bathroom were reconfigured, the latter with a skylight. A guest suite was created from a downstairs bedroom and bathroom. The garage was rebuilt, and good soil "that will actually sustain life" was trucked in. Rocks in the front of the house, reminders of Leschi's glacial landscape, echo the color of the painted cedar siding. While the front garden is "cottagey," says the woman of the house, the "masculine house wouldn't tolerate a really full-blown cottage garden."

"This is an extremely accommodating and flexible house that easily handles onslaughts of guests and large art projects," she adds. "The massive fireplace, the kitchen, and the generous front porch are all magnets for us and for our guests. We feel privileged to live in such a well-designed and welcoming house."

The exposed rafter tails of the roof and shed dormers combine with the porch's three H-shaped posts—an abundance of wood spilling its boundaries—to reinforce the 3,900-square-foot bungalow's Craftsman look (opposite, top). ▪ Window seats in the living room and elsewhere make the most of the house's views (bottom left). The floors are oak and the walls plaster with deep molding and Craftsman window surrounds. ▪ The kitchen, which the owners now liken to a butler's pantry, was bumped out two feet to allow space for an island and to maximize natural light (bottom right). A green tile backsplash running between the Arts and Crafts–style cabinets carries a subtle leaf motif. ▪ The Northwest's abundant supply of wood was tapped for the dining room's handsome fir paneling and sideboard with leaded-glass cabinets (below).

Drawn from below for the March 1916 cover of *Bungalow Magazine,* the entrance pergola looms even larger than life (above). Window boxes are built in below. ▪ Storey's Chicago roots no doubt gave him an affinity for Prairie-style hallmarks such as striking horizontality reinforced by sheltering eaves (right). ▪ In the living room some of the house's three dozen windows, marked in the corners with the Ellsworth Storey diagonal, usher in welcome sun (opposite). The Watts also finished their bungalow's basement with a family room, a guest bedroom, a bathroom, and a work room overlooking a Japanese garden.

SUPPLEMENT BUNGALOW WITH COMPLETE WORKING DRAWINGS, SPECIFICATIONS AND BILL OF MATERIAL

Cover Storey

Although this bungalow in Mount Baker might look like a refugee from California's sunnier climes, a little detective work would soon uncover the trademark of the noted local architect Ellsworth Storey. He left his signature in diagonal muntins bisecting the corners of the windows. With its lacy pergola held high on Brobdingnagian pillars, the three-bedroom speculative house gained local fame after it was featured on the cover of the March 1916 *Bungalow Magazine,* published in Seattle by Jud Yoho. Calling the house's simple treatment "an architectural lesson," the editors effused that it "has a fine setting into which it fits in a seductive fashion."

"Our house is more famous than we are!" laughs Vreni Watt, who has lived in the 2,500-square-foot house since 1986 but admits that the bungalow has "connected us with lots of people who are interested in historic houses such as this." Built in 1914, it was one of several bungalows Storey designed. A few years earlier he had begun an enclave of a dozen Western Stick Style cottages in Colman Park, now a Seattle landmark known as the Ellsworth Storey Cottages. The bold features of the modest stucco bungalow made it at home in its exclusive neighborhood of grand houses and Olmsted-designed roadways and parkland overlooking Lake Washington.

Given that they had to recreate the pergola as well as replace kitchen and other interior features long since removed, Vreni and Jerry Watt were grateful for the magazine's coverage. Detailed plans and photographs, all intended to spur readers to build their own Storey bungalow for about $3,200, proved invaluable in the restoration carried out by the couple's architect, Joseph Greif. Agreeing with *Bungalow Magazine's* criticism that the front pillars looked "far too massive for the light weight which they are expected to support," they chose to use columns more in scale with the overhead trellis. The Watts also discarded an earlier owner's green fiberglass canopy. Now clear glass keeps out the Seattle dew.

Glass doors in the rebuilt pantry cabinets repeat Storey's signature
triangular motif, creating a feathery pattern that recalls Frank Lloyd
Wright's nature-inspired Prairie art glass (left). The wooden cabinet
tucked into the alcove is a reminder of the owner's Swiss heritage.
Three bedrooms are located off the hallway. ▪ The Watts extracted a
period look for their bathroom even while retaining an array of Moderne
fixtures in celadon green that suited an earlier owner's taste (above).

Now You See It

Seattle's western peninsula fronting Puget Sound was long isolated from the city even though Alki Point there marked the site of Seattle's first brief nonnative settlement in 1851. Transportation limited to a "mosquito fleet" of steamships and the sidewheeler ferry *City of Seattle* kept West Seattle removed from city life into the 1880s. Occasional visitors, if not commuters, came out to stay in scattered resort communities. This shed-roof bungalow, built in 1906 on the cusp of the area's development, began life as one of West Seattle's summer cottages erected on land previously logged by the Yesler lumber empire.

Attracted by the location, a partial view of Puget Sound and the Olympic Mountains, a clinker-brick fireplace, and the original woodwork, never painted, the owners bought the 2,000-square-foot bungalow in 1989. Two renovations have been carried out with the help of their architect, Sharon Davidoff, and their interior designer, Laurie Taylor. First came the remodeling of a 1980s kitchen, and then the roof was raised to add a second bathroom and to reconfigure the three bedrooms upstairs. Next a family room at the back of the house was added over an enlarged basement.

A century has passed since the first tax assessment recorded the bungalow as being of "substandard construction." Bridges of various kinds have long since linked West Seattle to downtown, but the bungalow remains at the end of a six-house cul-de-sac on a street that is still unpaved. "We take great pleasure," say the owners, "in living on one of the last dirt roads in Seattle."

Siding ties together the large gabled dormer, the porch skirt, and the first floor, while the gable ends are shingled for contrast (opposite). Native plants in the yard were chosen to provide color year-round. ▪ Bungalow owners everywhere may be jealous of the house's space-saving Murphy bed, created by Wood Specialties (below left and right). Closed, it hides out as a fine cabinet in their downstairs guest room (originally the kitchen), veneered in quartersawn oak. When needed for guests, the doors open to reveal a queen-sized bed.

Shipshape

When Marsha Conn, an art teacher, moved into her West Seattle bungalow a decade ago, she knew that the muddled "Bad Room"—the kitchen—had to be fixed, but it took her seven years to decide how to do it. She and her architect, Tim Andersen, worked out a solution atypical of the usual Arts and Crafts kitchen remodeling. "I didn't want to have that dark, formal Craftsman kitchen everyone sees," she explained to *Seattle* magazine. For the new kitchen and den that would open onto a covered terrace Andersen had already added to the back, the two decided on something more casual and in tune with the natural wood, tinted white with white trim, used for the terrace. "That space is really an outdoor room," notes Andersen, "with its low-pitched gabled roof suspended in the treetops, framing a beautiful view of Puget Sound and the Olympics." Evoking a taut ship's galley, her kitchen now rests under a gently curved fir ceiling that masks uneven ceiling heights left after a wall was removed between rooms.

Conn's 1908 Craftsman bungalow was one of several in the neighborhood built by John Hanson—including a house for each of his three daughters—just a year after the arrival of the streetcar launched West Seattle's land boom of 1907. That same year the peninsula, Seattle's Plymouth Rock, gave up its political independence and became one of six towns annexed by Seattle. Residents still treasure their insularity and maintain an independent streak, down to periodic attempts to secede from the mother city.

Conn shares a similar passion for pursuing her own design style. The inviting front porch, which trails off into an arbor, first caught her eye. Inside the 2,800-square-foot bungalow awaited untouched box-beam ceilings, a rugged stone fireplace in the living room, and a dining room with a built-in fir sideboard and a plate rail atop tall wooden wainscoting. Other rooms include an entry hall, the new "little den," two guest bedrooms plus the master bedroom, two bathrooms, an office, and a studio. Now Conn has filled her home with a personalized collection of southern folk art, Native American artifacts, and pottery from Oaxaca. "Making a space that is comfortable," she says, "that is my aesthetic."

When the exterior siding was removed, cedar shingles were found beneath (opposite, top left). A rugged clinker-brick foundation and piers rise up to hold pairs of wooden porch supports; large braces support the low gabled roof. Stretched along the broad side gable above, five windows fill the shed-roof dormer. ▪ On the front porch is a wood and rattan swing that would have pleased Gustav Stickley (top right). An arbor overhead leaves half of the porch open to the fresh air. Puget Sound can be seen upstairs at the back of the house. ▪ The builder's three daughters all were married in front of the house's fireplace, over which is a 1930s painting of Mount Rainier by Louise Gilbert (bottom left). A fir divider separates the living and dining areas. ▪ Although the kitchen's curved bead-board ceiling was a challenge for the builders, it gave the space the cozy feel of a boathouse (bottom right).

Counterbalance

Queen Anne Hill's steep slopes—topping out at 456 feet above Puget Sound—slowed its initial development and then its completion as one of Seattle's most desirable residential districts. Finally in 1902 an electric trolley line made its way up the eighteen-degree grade of Queen Anne Avenue, thanks to a system of counterweights that controlled the cars from below street level. This streetcar nicknamed Counterbalance opened the way for houses at the crest and along the south side, affording views of Mount Rainier and Elliott Bay.

Bungalows like this 1916 Craftsman at the top of the hill soon mixed in with the Queen Anne–style houses that had brought about the area's name change from Eden Hill. Judy Cherin bought the shingled 5,000-square-foot bungalow in 1985, charmed by its simplicity and the fact that it had never been painted inside, even though the original owner had lived here for nearly seventy years. Wood used for built-in bookcases, the dining room buffet, wainscoting, and crown molding is all old-growth fir.

With the architectural services of Clinton Miller and interior design advice from Laurie Taylor, she has enlarged the kitchen, incorporating a small back porch and using vertical-grain fir to match the woodwork already in the house; remodeled the upstairs bathroom in period style; and finished the house with appropriate Arts and Crafts furnishings. An exterior wall with gates complementing the house was executed by Daniel Yarger Designs in 1996, and the basement has been converted into a one-bedroom apartment. Like the Queen Anne streetcar, the house's original vision has achieved a delicate balance, melding the builder's vision with the modern need for refuge. Now when Cherin and Barbara Griffin walk through their gate, "Life doesn't follow you in the door," they marvel.

Battered brick piers, their verticality contrasting with the horizontality of the porch siding, hold aloft an arcaded apron framing the front gable (above). ▪ Inset with art glass in a Mackintosh-like floral pattern, a pair of new fir gates that open off a wall offer privacy on a busy street (opposite). The pergola's exaggerated stickwork mirrors motifs from the house itself. Beyond is a back-yard habitat furnished with two fountains amid indigenous plants.

A landscape frieze in the dining room and willow wallpaper in the living room, both from Bradbury and Bradbury, make quiet backgrounds for the owners' period furnishings and collections of Native American and western art and crafts (left). The dining room set from the early 1900s is by Berkey Gay. ▪ A consignment-store pew with echoes of Frank Lloyd Wright anchors one wall of the living room (top right). Another bargain was the tabouret table, which holds a Lorelei pot by Van Briggle beneath Beth Van Hoesen's rooster, *Boris.* The original push-button switches remain in working order. ▪ The upstairs bathroom was completely redone in period style using recycled fixtures. Subway tile on the walls and hexagonal floor tiles make a sanitary white backdrop for a clawfoot tub, a pedestal sink, and an old toilet (bottom right).

New Lease on Life

In a burst of patriotic fever after Theodore Roosevelt died in 1919, a section of northeast Seattle near the Ravenna district on Union Bay was renamed for the president and Tenth Avenue became Roosevelt Way. By then both the Roosevelt and Ravenna neighborhoods, served by streetcar beginning in 1891, had already seen a bungalow boom. As the University of Washington expanded over the years, the area's bungalows just to the north attracted many faculty, students, and staff.

This 1915 shed-roof bungalow two blocks off Roosevelt Way in Cowen's University Park saw its share of student renters from 1976 to 1995, when it was purchased by David and Penny Eckert. They have been working steadily ever since to erase the scars of those years. Under the guidance of their architect, Alexandra Gorny, the front porch was re-built, the kitchen and upstairs bathroom were remodeled, the back porch was removed and a new deck constructed, and a powder room and a solarium were added. Plans call for redoing the upstairs, which has three bedrooms and a full bathroom; improving the closets; and completing a basement apartment that brings the bungalow's area to about 3,450 square feet.

"The kitchen, with its open solarium and friendly connection to the rest of the house, has become the center of family activities," says Penny. "From a dark, gloomy, and inconvenient necessity, the kitchen has been transformed into a comfortable and friendly space. Our teenagers will now invite their friends over and are no longer embarrassed by their run-down home!"

The porch was restored with tongue-and-groove fir, retaining the original trim and column trios anchoring each side above the battered piers (below). Shingles in the side gables flare out over built-up trim bands. Leaded glass fills the upper lights of the front windows. ▪ To open up the space between the dining room and the kitchen, Alexandra Gorny designed a handsome built-in buffet of Douglas fir (right). Pass-through leaded-glass cabinet doors, lighted inside, echo the windows and can be accessed from either side.

Front Row Seat

One of the massive public works projects that transformed Seattle into a world-class city early in the twentieth century was the Lake Washington Ship Canal. Finally constructed between 1911 and 1917 although first suggested several decades earlier, the route linked Lake Washington with Lake Union and then Puget Sound. This cottagelike bungalow in the Montlake area of northeast Seattle, built about a year after the canal was completed, originally enjoyed a view of the new industrial waterway that a later owner for some reason blocked with a detached garage at the back of the house.

When Chris and Jasmine Bryant moved in, they called in the Johnson Partnership to fix their view. Larry Johnson and Howard Miller put the garage below grade, as it had been originally, but connected it to the house and made room for a patio on top. They also improved the cramped floor plan by merging two small bedrooms into an expanded open kitchen with fir cabinets and a family room looking out over the patio. The old kitchen with its breakfast nook was made into a bedroom. In the attic, which includes two bedrooms and a bathroom, the back bedroom opens onto a balcony built for two with an elevated view of the canal. The basement contains a media room.

Home to the University of Washington baseball coach Dorsett "Tubby" Graves from 1923 to 1946, the 3,000-square-foot house has other ties to local history. Excavation for the garage uncovered a telephone conduit that apparently served as a major trunk line for the Alaska-Yukon-Pacific Exposition of 1909. This fair, promoting Seattle's role as a gateway to Alaska, was held across the ship canal where the university stands today. For the exposition, the Olmsted Brothers created a classical site plan on axis with Mount Rainier, a feature retained by the university. Today the Seattle Museum of History and Industry, which is in the same neighborhood, displays a piece of the historic conduit.

Both owners attended college in Pasadena and "loved the bungalow style" before finding the house. "We had made several trips to the Gamble House and are admirers of Greene and Greene's craftsmanship," explain the Bryants. With the remodeling complete and the paint removed from the woodwork, the house, they conclude, "just feels like us."

The jerkinhead (clipped) gables convey a medieval look, while the small entry portico is a Victorian vestige (above). Like a shallow visor, a shed roof continues around past the porch to shelter the front windows. ▪ An Arts and Crafts serenity prevails in the remodeled kitchen and the dining room, which is furnished with reproduction spindle-back chairs and a sideboard (opposite). Forest green paint on the plaster walls provides a woodsy background between the original oak floors and the added plate rail.

Wright Angles

Frank Lloyd Wright did not design a house in the Seattle area until 1945, but with the westward emigration of two draftsmen from his studio in Oak Park, Illinois, his ideas preceded him. Andrew Willatsen and Barry Byrne joined together in 1909 as Willatsen and Byrne and began to add the Prairie style to Seattle's architectural palette. With its broad eaves, generous bands of windows, sheltered porch, and easy relationship with the outdoors, this modest Prairie house built in 1912 shares the qualities that made bungalows so attractive. Its rectangular plan of living room, dining room, and kitchen downstairs and three bedrooms plus one bathroom (now two) upstairs echoes that of many bungalows nationwide.

George and Grace Bellman paid $10 down for the $3,500 house, on which workers were forbidden from using "profane language." Bellman wrote movie reviews for the *Seattle Sun,* visiting with Hollywood luminaries at William Randolph Hearst's San Simeon to get in a congenial frame of mind. The Great Depression brought about the house's foreclosure, but relatives of past owners have returned over the years.

Jim Williamson, a designer and illustrator, and Dabney Benjamin, an artist and woodworker, purchased the house in 1991. Its legacy and its Montlake location sold them, but the birth of their two children in the house has cemented their attachment to it. First came the basics: a new roof and gutters, chimney repairs, and new paint for the front door. Next they tackled the knottier problem of fixing the kitchen, redone by an earlier owner. For inspiration they reached back to the homey kitchens Benjamin remembered from her two grandmothers' homes, visiting them to measure and photograph cabinets and fixtures to get the details right. But the chance find of a 1930s Wedgewood stove made everything fall into place. Then Williamson, who had researched Willatsen's papers at the University of Washington, designed a central island that serves as a work surface as well as a kitchen table.

Encouraged by how the kitchen turned out, the couple renovated the two upstairs bathrooms (one originally a closet) to give them an early-twentieth-century look from tilework to appropriate fixtures and lighting. Says Williamson, "The magic is in the details." This is a lesson that Willatsen and Byrne, who went their separate ways a year after designing this house, learned at Wright's drawing board.

Despite the house's two full stories, the horizontal line predominates (below). Bevelled siding stretches across the front and onto the flat roof of the porch, which shelters the side entrance. The contrasting stucco band above tends to make the wall disappear, thus shifting visual weight to the ground floor. Windows are grouped to serve as the eyes of the house, as Wright would have liked. In its overall appearance, the house recalls the many "Classic Boxes" found in Seattle. ▪ To get the look of freestanding furniture, Dabney Benjamin fashioned legs for the kitchen's maple cabinets to echo the stove and recessed the kick space (opposite). New windows and skylights now reflect the scale of other windows in the house.

Their Favorite Things

I n a city where mountains loom so large, it was almost inevitable—
and absolutely fitting—that the bungalow's chalet roots would show
themselves here. Seattle's noted architect Ellsworth Storey returned
from a European trip with a fondness for Swiss chalets that emerged
a decade later in this 1909 bungalow in Denny Blaine. It was one of two
neighboring houses designed by Storey that William Brehm, a builder,
constructed for himself and his brother George, a merchant at Pike
Place Market. With its rustic materials and steep gabled roof, it fit comfortably into the hilly subdivision alongside Lake Washington that was
developed beginning in 1901 by Charles L. Denny and Elbert F. Blaine.

The owners found what they call their "cabin in the woods" after living first in a bungalow in Wallingford that grew too small for their expanding family and then in a Queen Anne that proved impossible to
fix. They were fortunate that the previous owner, Roy McMakin, was
a furniture designer who replaced wood features and installed a period
kitchen and an upstairs bathroom. The house's three bedrooms are also
in the upper space.

Remodelings from past decades and an upstairs fire had left the 2,500-
square-foot house in need of loving care, although the elaborate fir
woodwork had remained unscathed. Beginning with the outside, rotting rafters, gutters, knee braces, and a bargeboard were replaced at
the back of the house. All the patching meant that the house then had
to be stained. A nondescript garage was sided and detailed to match
the house. The owners' hope is that
they can "pass it along to someone
else in a little bit better condition
than when we got it."

"The brilliance of Ellsworth Storey's
design," they reflect, "is its simplicity. During the winter months, it is
very light in here, and in the summer
it's very shady and cool because of
the way he designed the eaves for the
height of the sun. He was an engineer
in that way."

A massive granite chimney anchors the house,
which is clad in fir, and also announces its
presence on a broad front porch (below).
Untamed landscaping heightens the romantic
effect. ▪ The dining room shows off the house's
distinctive woodwork, which includes board-
and-batten fir wainscoting as well as bracketed
ceiling beams (opposite). ▪ Horizontal and
vertical, light and dark, rough granite and silky
oiled fir—Storey skillfully used architectural
contrasts to add energy to the living room
(overleaf). In the pair of French doors beneath
H-shaped lintels can be seen his signature:
diagonal muntins bisecting the corners.

Pumped-Up Bungalow

The Seattle suburb of Medina, on the eastern shore of Lake Washington, is home to McMansions built by technology wizards, but the tour buses drive by to gawk at a lakeside vestige there from an earlier age. Except that what its architect, Alexandra Gorny, calls a "pumped-up bungalow" is not old. A great command of Arts and Crafts principles and carefully researched details combined at the beginning of the twenty-first century to produce a bungalow as genuine as one conceived at the start of the twentieth.

The project began with the goal of building a "completely American" house, one that would expand on the French-born owner's newfound fascination with the Arts and Crafts movement. This software industry professional made a pilgrimage to Pasadena and then took a year and a half off to devote all her energies to researching the proper woodwork, hardware, tile, lighting, curtains, wallpaper, and other features, insisting on the best artisans and suppliers. Gorny, who at the time was the project architect for Curtis Gelotte, melded the owner's preferences with Gelotte's plan to finish the 4,400-square-foot house in a refined bungalow style.

Securely of its place even if purposely out of time, the reinterpreted Craftsman uses typical local materials from granite to cedar siding and trim to copper gutters, with a forest of sensuous Douglas fir inside. Pilasters of fir frame the overscaled living room fireplace, whose surround and hearth show off plain and patterned tiles. Japanese features slide easily into the Arts and Crafts sensibility, reappearing in a tansu storage unit tucked under the stairs and the design of the master bathroom. Gorny, a bungalow owner herself, relished the collaborative process but does not encourage new developer-built bungalow knockoffs. "Most builders of brand-new homes," she told *American Bungalow* readers, "don't have the budget to really pay attention to the details."

The bungalow's two full stories over a lighted basement are masked by its low scale at the front of a sloping lot (above). The pair of gabled dormers and the gabled porch are mirrored at the back. ▪ The stairway was inspired by one in a 1907 California house designed by Louis Christian Mullgardt, while the built-in stair-stepped Japanese tansu chest was modeled after one the owner saw in the book *American Bungalow Style* (opposite).

The Pacific Northwest's distinctive board-and-batten fir wainscoting makes a rich background for the Arts and Crafts furnishings, most of which came from contemporary suppliers (opposite). Laurie Taylor of Ivy Hill Interiors served as the interior designer. ▪ A colonnaded divider fashioned of vertical-cut fir and inset with leaded-glass doors breaks up the large floor area into intimate spaces recalling those in its bungalow predecessors (right).

Mr. Blandings Redux?

If the movies *Mr. Blandings Builds His Dream House* or *The Money Pit* come to mind when hearing Scott and Darby Johnson talk about their bungalow, they would not be surprised. In buying one of the few bungalows to come on the market in Kirkland, across Lake Washington, they bought a pack of troubles in 1996. For starters, it had been moved six blocks uphill three years earlier and set on a new foundation. When built in 1916 as a vacation cottage, the shed-roof bungalow had a waterfront location with exceptional views, but the waterfront was soon relocated three blocks west when the ship canal lowered the lake's water level.

"I wanted a house I could work on," says Scott, adding, "which I got in spades." Everything in the living room had been painted white, including the clinker-brick fireplace and the crosscut Douglas fir paneling. One of the couple's first tasks was to restore the fireplace. "Darby wasn't happy with the work done on the firebox," relates Scott, "so she called another masonry contractor." What he found was that there was no foundation to support five tons of brick. Out came the chimney and in went a wood-burning insert. Other discrepancies were found between the approved plans and the actual postmove reconstruction—matters having to do with structural integrity.

After the big problems were fixed, the usual restoration work began: stripping, sanding, staining, and replacing woodwork; removing drywall that covered the plaster walls and then repairing the plaster; repairing windows and installing storm windows; adding French doors to close off the sun porch from the living room; and installing period lighting. "We can look at a Christmas picture and tell what year it was by the location of the tarp," explains Scott.

The couple and their two children finally have time to enjoy their 3,500-square-foot bungalow, which includes a reconstructed master bedroom on the first floor, two bedrooms upstairs and two in the basement, a formal dining room added in the 1940s, three bathrooms, a first-floor office, an open television room upstairs, and a garage. Arbitration brought about "semivindication" for the structural problems, "although our pocketbook ended up feeling semivacant," laughs Scott. Just don't ask him about what happened when he removed a dead tree.

Half of the porch was closed in long ago to make a sunroom, and in the 1930s the original cedar siding was covered with cedar shingles (opposite, top left). "We use the porch every day in the summer," say the Johnsons. "We eat meals there, visit with neighbors, and just hang out." ▪ The clinker brick was cleaned of its paint, but the chimney had to be replaced with a vented wood-burning insert to reduce the structural load on the house (top right). The hearth was retiled after it was reconstructed. ▪ Fir cut across the grain frames a large arched window and meanders around the room in wainscoting, a plate rail, and window surrounds (bottom). The interior designer Karen Hovde has provided the Johnsons with design assistance as they refurnish their home.

Looking Backward

Can a couple who have lived for fifteen years in an old Craftsman bungalow in Seattle find happiness in a new bungalow out on Bainbridge Island along Puget Sound's western shore? Tanya and Eric Clauson could and did, after an intervening attempt at housekeeping in a former church. As a reminder of the 1917 bungalow they had loved so much, they were able to adopt the old neighborhood's name—Magnolia—as the name of their new bungalow.

The name was actually bestowed by the architect of their new home, Christian Gladu, who decided some years ago that he would rather design cozy new bungalows than the larger houses on which he had been working. Now, following in the footsteps of the planbook publishers who sparked a bungalow boom in Seattle a century ago, Gladu has launched the Bungalow Company to supply well-thought-out, individualized houses melding old and new. "It's about taking what happened originally and reinterpreting it for today with available materials that are appropriate for the region," he noted in *American Bungalow*.

The Clausons' 2,500-square-foot bungalow was built in an enclave of other backward-looking homes by craftsmen who feel the same way as Gladu. David and Irving Spellman of Spellman Construction completed the three-bedroom, two-and-one-half-bathroom house in 1998. In addition to the entry, living and dining rooms, study, and kitchen downstairs, the classically styled bungalow connects via a breezeway with a two-car garage that has a home office above.

David Spellman takes fellow builder-developers to task for advertising new houses as Craftsman. "I feel like the term has been cheapened. Now I refuse to call my homes that; I'll call them bungalows but not Craftsmans."

The exterior was carefully crafted with all the right bungalow details: cedar siding and shakes, battered wood porch columns atop used-brick piers, stucco arches, exposed rafter tails, and a large shingled dormer with an openwork bargeboard and dentil molding under the gabled roof (top). ▪ "Why they ever went out of style," says Tanya Clauson about her breakfast nook, "I can't imagine" (bottom). ▪ The Clausons personalized their new bungalow with jewel-like leaded-glass windows designed by Peter Schaefer flanking the fireplace as well as the front door (opposite).

Bigger, Better

The sad little bungalow in Port Townsend might not have extracted a second glance from most people, but Colby Fox had an eye attuned to finding the hidden charms of old houses. And besides, the view out over a bluff toward the Strait of Juan de Fuca, capped by a distant Mount Baker, was impossible to pass up. So in 1990 she bought the house—built in the early 1900s for General John Hayden, the commander of Fort Worden—together with two of its original three lots.

Down came the aluminum siding, to be replaced by shingles, and out came the walls by as much as eight feet in places. The front door was moved; the porch grew bigger, with recycled siding used for its ceiling; and a quartet of larger dormers replaced the single dormer with which the bungalow started out. The old cinder-block foundation was reinforced, and a new one was laid under the expanded portion. Doors and trim of Douglas fir were refinished and replaced where needed. The architectural work was done by Ann Landis, and Fox's friend Edward Morgan served as a sounding board for design ideas.

Fox scavenged for doors and missing features to avoid using reproductions wherever possible. While awaiting their new bungalow, she and her housemate, Mary Morrissey, lived in a small cottage on the property for two years. After the work was finished, Fox was relieved when a neighbor exclaimed over the new old bungalow: "It's like you've given a gift to the community."

The back of the house, seen from the garden room's stone wall, shows two of the four new dormers built to allow a spacious master suite upstairs (opposite, top left). Inspiration for the cement-capped fieldstone chimney came from bungalows along the Oregon coast. ▪ The yard has taken on a naturalized look, with Japanese maples, spreading evergreens, and ferns lining gravel paths, all framed by three twenty-foot firs (top right). ▪ To take advantage of the view, the dining room was extended into the original pantry and a new fir-lined pantry took the place of a bedroom in which the general's houseboy once slept (bottom left). ▪ A clawfoot tub moved from downstairs is the focal point of the new attic bathroom, whose vanity was fashioned from an old dry sink (bottom right). ▪ A fireplace featured in *American Bungalow* gave Fox the idea for her own hearth, pieced together from hand-collected stones that tumble naturally toward the ground (right).

THE TWIN CITIES

"Even in Minnesota's harsh climate, bungalows have proven to be exceptionally sturdy homes," observes Mary Reichardt, owner of a St. Paul bungalow shown in the following pages. That the Twin Cities of Minneapolis and St. Paul became the first major midwestern region to wholeheartedly embrace the bungalow is due in no small part to their own geography. The only natural waterfall on the Mighty Mississippi, which divides the two cities, unleashed an unparalleled source of power that early settlers in the nineteenth century tapped to produce lumber and mill flour. To work the mills, many of them established by easterners, came Swedes and other Scandinavians as well as German and Irish immigrants. And to house them and workers who ran the railroads and laid the streetcar lines, bungalows that could be turned out on a few basic plans fit the bill.

The years 1904–5 were a watershed time for the bungalow movement in Minneapolis (meaning "city of the waters," incorporated in 1856) and St. Paul (named after a French church as an improvement on its previous name, Pig's Eye, and incorporated in 1849). Minnesota, with St. Paul its capital, had entered the union in 1858. While Minneapolis evolved into an industrial giant, St. Paul became a political and business center filled with sought-after Victorian neighborhoods and more modest working-class suburbs. Citizens viewed themselves as residents of an American Arcadia—a democratic, egalitarian society nourishing a vibrant urban middle class off the bounty of the land, according to the cultural geographer James R. Shortridge. The Arts and Crafts ideals of proponents such as William Morris and Gustav Stickley found a welcome home here. Newcomers of European descent joined the search for simplicity and naturalness in their homes and everyday lives. One of the country's earliest Arts and Crafts organizations, the Chalk and Chisel Club, was formed in 1895 and was soon renamed the Society of Arts and Crafts of Minneapolis.

Macalester-Groveland in St. Paul, one of the Twin Cities' numerous bungalow neighborhoods, is like a small town within the city. Streetcars ferried commuters to work and back early in the twentieth century.

By 1939 rows of simple bungalows such as these on the east side of Arthur Street, N.E., near Twenty-sixth Street in Minneapolis filled Twin Cities neighborhoods. Front gables create a straightforward look.

In 1904 Stickley visited the Twin Cities, meeting with the local designer John S. Bradstreet, whose work he found "worthy to initiate a national movement." That same year *Keith's Magazine,* published from Minneapolis between 1899 and 1931, extolled the small house: "The happiness of the home depends almost entirely on the fit. It is much more difficult to make a large house cozy than a small one, and a house to be comfortable must be cozy," admonished this publisher of architectural advice and construction plans. The next year the city's Arts and Crafts society was renamed the Handicraft Guild, offering courses in pottery, metalwork, interior decoration, and related crafts training. The noted tilemaker Ernest Batchelder taught design and theory at the guild for four years beginning in 1905, influencing a generation of local Arts and Crafts enthusiasts and teachers.

By 1912 *Keith's* could proudly proclaim, "There are two cities in the United States noted for the unusual merit of their small houses—Pasadena, Cal., and Minneapolis, Minn." In addition to featuring grand Arts and Crafts homes for readers to emulate, the magazine sold bungalow plans so that workers in the Twin Cities and elsewhere could build affordable yet cozy homes of their own. The region's lumberyards and its skilled immigrant carpenters and builders coalesced to plant bungalows in neighborhoods such as Minneapolis's Longfellow—named after Henry Wadsworth Longfellow's "Song of Hiawatha," describing the city's Minnehaha Falls—and St. Paul's Macalester-Groveland, a streetcar suburb that grew up on the river bluffs in the late 1910s and the 1920s.

Some of these small homes came from Sears, but most were homegrown. Would-be homeowners could go to one of the many lumberyards downtown and pick a house from a planbook, explains Kristi Lee Johnson, founder of the Twin Cities Bungalow Club. Then the company's contractors or an independent builder chose which of the milled and dried oak or white pine floated downriver from the North Woods would make the best bungalow. "The old-growth white pine was stronger than steel," says Johnson. Horse-drawn wagons pulled the

lumber and millwork to the building site for construction. Carpenter-builders also speculated in bungalows, buying neighboring lots and sequentially building on them—often moving their families from one bungalow to another as each was finished. By 1914, when the national bungalow boom was in full swing, Minneapolis was second only to San Francisco in housing starts, and a good percentage were bungalows.

Twin Cities bungalows were typically built to standardized plans and materials, avoiding waste and thereby pleasing the Scandinavian soul. They tend to be a fairly plain box with several jewels inside. Local bungalows' unpretentious exteriors—perhaps stucco under a simple gabled roof with half-timbering to convey the right medieval touch—divulge richly appointed Arts and Crafts interiors that no cabinetmaker could be ashamed of. Porches are enclosed for three-season use or, with the addition of sufficient heating, for enjoyment in the winter as well. Spring is announced by lovingly tended gardens that expand the livability of the typical 950- or 1,200-square-foot bungalow.

By the late twentieth century the Twin Cities' bungalows had gained a reputation as "starter homes" that were not worth saving. "To me, it implied that you were supposed to move on," says Johnson. Code requirements discouraging renovation reinforced this view. The formation of the Twin Cities Bungalow Club in 1996 brought about a sea change in attitude and engendered pride in bungalow origins (a claim even Minnesota's recent wrestling governor, Jesse Ventura, could make). A building code modification has grandfathered in the original steep bungalow stairways, so that owners who want to expand into their upper half stories can do so. The Longfellow neighborhood, where Johnson began the club, has published a remodeling guide showing homeowners how to update in historically appropriate ways. Twin Cities bungalows and their neighborhoods are now avidly sought after. "All the principles of the New Urbanism," says Johnson, "have been happily working in bungalow neighborhoods for generations."

Without the open porches found in other regions, Twin Cities bungalow owners lavish care on their window boxes, many of which are built in (bottom left). ▪ Even if they are plain outside, local bungalows hold treasures inside. The built-in oak buffet in Dennis Williams's stucco house in the Longfellow neighborhood of Minneapolis, added after the house was built in 1915, warms up the interior year-round (bottom right).

Purse-Strings Perfection

The Minneapolis writer Tim Counts knows a good bungalow when he sees one (the second president of the Twin Cities Bungalow Club, he helped locate the Twin Cities houses shown in this book). He has also learned firsthand how to bring a bungalow back to life and furnish it on a budget similar to ones followed by the first owners early in the twentieth century. He chose his own 1,100-square-foot, two-bedroom bungalow in the Corcoran neighborhood "primarily because it was in my price range, but also because words such as 'cozy' and 'charming' came to mind the first time I walked through," he told readers of *American Bungalow*.

Counts had to furnish his 1926 bungalow, a project that took five years, and deal with the "mess of a kitchen" he found. For the furnishings, he relied on antiques dealers and scouts to help him find second-tier items right for the period—they did not have to be Stickley or Limbert, for example, and a repaired Weller pot or a lucky-find painting worked just fine. "The original bungalow dwellers had a mix of furniture," he reasons, "most likely pieces from the Victorian era that had been handed down."

The kitchen proved an especially knotty problem, although it retained a picture-perfect breakfast nook and a wall of built-in cabinets. "To be truthful," Counts explains, "I'm not a fan of kitchen mega-makeovers that turn what was built as a utilitarian room into a theatrical experience—especially in a modest house." He decided to think small: an old midsize Frigidaire and a 24-inch-wide Windsor gas stove from the 1920s but no dishwasher. He had some new cabinets built to complement the originals and eventually settled on a linoleum counter edged with an aluminum strip. "Although my kitchen might be considered under-equipped for a gourmet chef or a large family," says Counts, "it functions quite well for what's demanded of it. In the process of updating it, a bit of domestic history was saved, not to mention a bundle of cash."

A distinctively troweled stucco covers the exterior of Counts's double-gabled bungalow, whose roof ends flush with the walls rather than in overhanging eaves (opposite, top left). Both the louvered vent on the porch gable and the decorative tiles above the upstairs windows are rare in the Twin Cities. The awning and light are new. ▪ In the office created on the porch just inside the door (top right), Counts shows off the tools of his trade: a 1917 typewriter purchased for $32 alongside a laptop computer. The chair is an Arts and Crafts find. ▪ A more regal Arts and Crafts chair in the living room needed only new upholstery (bottom). The gramophone cabinet makes a good home for a television and a VCR.

Tim Counts's original breakfast nook is probably the envy of any bungalow owner without one (left). The soft golden tones of the kitchen's walls blend subtly with the pale mint green chosen for the cabinets—brighter colors that were fashionable in the mid-1920s, when the bungalow was built.

The original wall-hung sink-drainboard combination was long since gone, so Counts installed a stainless-steel counter and sink over cabinets (above). The antique stove's green color proved an inspiration for repainting the kitchen.

Starter Home

At a cozy 950 square feet, Michael Damon and Tom Melmer's front-gabled home in the Longfellow neighborhood epitomizes Minneapolis's typical bungalow. On signs posted throughout the neighborhood, which stretches along the Mississippi River near the city's southern edge, Longfellow has declared itself a "Traditional Bungalow Community." Not long ago, however, its bungalows—more than half of the neighborhood's houses—were considered little more than starter homes, a stereotype the Twin Cities Bungalow Club has set out to change.

The bungalow's stucco has been painted white and the trim red, green, and beige to reflect Arts and Crafts color ideals, but the owners have changed little else in the one-story, two-bedroom house. It was the woodwork that first drew them in, as it does in so many of the Twin Cities' otherwise simple bungalows. Beneath an oak mantel, bookcases built of oak with glass doors flank the rectilinear brick fireplace in the living room, matched by an oak buffet in the dining room. The kitchen had been completely remodeled by some of the six previous owners but is soon to be put right.

Today both neighbors and strangers compliment the owners on how cute their bungalow is. Cascading plants in the flower box outside fulfill bungalow pioneers' visions of vine-covered cottages to come. As the Minneapolis-based *Keith's* magazine wrote in 1916, "The bungalow ... suggests the close to nature movement from its vine hung porches to its outdoor sleeping rooms. ..." Damon and Melmer concur, adding, "Bungalows are the perfect house for long Minnesota winters. It's great to sit by the fireplace and watch the snow come down!"

The entrance porch, with its gabled roof mimicking the main roof, was enclosed early on (top). ▪ **In the summer, morning glories twined around the picket fence lend an even more pastoral note to the bungalow's lush garden (center).** ▪ **The deep finish on an old Victrola owned by Damon's great-grandfather melds into the wood tones of the dining room's oak floors and trim (bottom). The custom rug from Marshall Field's, where Damon works, recalls the Scottish designer Charles Rennie Mackintosh.** ▪ **A plein-air painting (ca. 1915–20) by the Czech artist Josef Konecny and a collection of Roseville, Van Briggle, and other Arts and Crafts pottery make the living room fireplace glow even without a fire (opposite).**

Bungalow Two Step

Several years ago Lisa Selness and Kevin Johnson went looking for an unremodeled bungalow with its features still intact, "and we found it!" exclaims Selness. Their one-and-one-half-story home in Minneapolis's Longfellow neighborhood was built in 1924 for about $4,195 by David Hendrickson, a carpenter who lived in it for three years. Lots here in what was originally called Seven Oaks Acres were sold by the developer Edmund G. Walton for $425 to $500 in 1914. Although owned by at least a half dozen families since it was built—including a teacher, a Western Union employee, and an engineer—the front-gabled bungalow survived with few major modifications, "which is exactly why we purchased it," says Selness.

The simple stucco exterior belies the craftsmanship found inside the small house, whose footprint is just 902 square feet. Flattened ogee-curve arches of deep red oak, crowned with a keystone, frame the entrances into the living and dining rooms. Window surrounds and doors were also made of the same oak, as was the wall-to-wall built-in buffet in the dining room. Floors are oak in the public rooms, maple in the bedrooms and back hallway. The owners refinished the floors, removing one layer of linoleum in the kitchen to uncover 1930s commercial-grade linoleum in a geometric pattern underneath and a maple hardwood floor beneath that.

"We take pride in preserving the integrity of our old home," admit Selness and Johnson. They are antiques collectors who have made a point of seeking out period sheet music with bungalow themes, including Richard L. Weaver's "Bungalow Two Step" (1909) and Sophie Tucker's "He's Got a Bungalow" (1916). "We love living here because it offers us quality materials and design, efficient use of space, and coziness—which new homes in our price range simply do not offer."

Wood trim parcels the stucco front gable into sections aligned with the three upstairs windows (top). ▪ **The owners' changes began at the front door, which was replaced with a vintage door holding beveled glass matching the windows in the rest of the house (bottom).** ▪ **An accommodating double-back Arts and Crafts settle was found in an antiques store (opposite). Some of the owners' bungalow music collection from the early twentieth century is displayed here and in the dining room.**

A red oak archway announces the richly appointed dining room, with its oak buffet built into a windowed bay (right); the four pots at the far end are Roycroft reproductions. Ringed beneath a Colonial Revival light fixture are Mission-style dining chairs made in the early 1900s by the Wisconsin Chair Company of Port Washington, Wisconsin.

The original owner enshrined his newfangled telephone in an elegant alcove framed in red oak (above). Underneath an old fan, the radiator is concealed behind a spindled oak enclosure. The charcoal photograph is of Lisa Selness's great-grandfather, Fred Selness.

The Jewel of Seward

No doubt the iridescent, jewel-like chandelier in the dining room would have been enough to earn this bungalow its nickname, the "Jewel of Seward." But Robert Burgett and Clete Strak's home, located in Minneapolis's Seward neighborhood, most likely gained its name from the glowing combination of its rich woodwork, its corner location on a double lot with a view of the Mississippi River and St. Paul, and its precious Japanese garden crowned with a koi pond. Seward is the northernmost portion of Longfellow, abutting neighborhoods around the University of Minnesota.

A lush Arts and Crafts interior like those that typically await behind the city's restrained midwestern facades attracted Burgett and Strak when they purchased the house in 1998 following the death of the original owner's granddaughter. The large bungalow (4,000 square feet) with three bedrooms upstairs, built about 1913, "needed T.L.C.," they say. But its oak woodwork in the front rooms and maple in the back, lighting fixtures, and handmade leaded-glass doors were all original and basically in "impeccable condition."

The owners refinished the floors, updated the kitchen and bathroom, and stripped walls on the second floor that were "covered with 1920s cabbage rose pink wallpaper (yes, all of them)." After repainting in more period-appropriate colors and indulging their passion for early-twentieth-century antiques and collectibles such as Czech art glass, they have made this jewel of a bungalow "perfect for entertaining family and friends."

Intersecting front- and side-facing gables, together with a mix of materials—brick, stucco, and wood—enliven the exterior (top). Tudoresque stickwork and exaggerated knee braces add to the bungalow's charm. ▪ The simple, free-flowing forms of the traditional Japanese garden were models for Arts and Crafts landscape designers. Here koi were used to create a golden necklace in the bungalow's pond (center). ▪ A Tiffany-style copper chandelier with Favrile glass glows, jewel-like, against the box-beam ceiling (bottom). ▪ Protecting early-twentieth-century Czech art glass like glazed vitrines, the built-in glass-front oak cases and buffet frame the Arts and Crafts dining room (opposite).

Home Office

I f it is true that you can't tell a book by its cover, then Bill and Linda Lundborg's 1923 home in Linden Hills is the perfect roost for a pair of book designers. Open the door under the double-gabled entrance and a sensuous Arts and Crafts tale unfolds inside, written in simple lines and illustrated with rich color. Since the owners turned the attic into their graphic design studio, they can look down from their workday loft into the living area below. Its ceiling removed, the living room now reaches up dramatically to the rooftop. The Lundborgs have also added a great room at the back of their house, enlarged the kitchen, and built a deck onto their two-bedroom bungalow.

Their home office is just steps from Lake Harriet (named for the wife of a colonel assigned to Fort Snelling in the Minnesota Territory), not far from downtown Minneapolis. Native Americans once lived around the three-mile-wide lake. By the turn of the twentieth century, a succession of large pavilions provided food and entertainment to city residents carried out on the streetcar line—a remnant of which still keeps Minneapolitans in touch with the lake, one of the Twin Cities' many outdoor rooms. Active in the Linden Hills History Study Group, the couple designed its award-winning neighborhood history book.

After two and a half decades in their bungalow, the Lundborgs' favorite rooms remain the living room and the enclosed front porch. "We have purposely kept the exterior of the house quite simple," they confess. "It's fun to watch people's reactions as they come inside." The same can be said of many Twin Cities bungalows that hide a heart of gold behind a plain-Jane exterior.

Tudoresque detailing distinguishes the double gables in the Lundborgs' stucco bungalow (bottom left). The cottagelike porch features a bead-board ceiling, a wide-board floor, and swing-open windows. ▪ Just inside, the colors in the living room deepen to woodsy Arts and Crafts tones inspired by the oak woodwork and maple floors (bottom right). Spindle-back chairs from Stickley create an intimate seating area, lighted by a Van Erp reproduction lamp with a mica shade. The blown-glass fish is Venetian. ▪ The opened-up living room (opposite) is furnished in "Stickley with a twist," including rattan and Morris chairs and other reproduction pieces beneath a thrift-store statue whose paint was removed. The deep moss green plaster walls have the patina of aged leather and make the quartet of Edward Curtis Indian photographs pop from the wall.

Living Simply and Well

The previous owner—"a notorious south Minneapolis bag lady, with twenty cats and two Dobermans"—left this 1919 Kingfield bungalow in rough shape and the yard "dark and dank," according to the house's current, and third, owners, Richard Rueter and Raymond Dillon. Because Rueter had owned and loved a Craftsman bungalow for twenty years, they took on the challenge of this "fixer-upper that had much of its original charm." Kingfield began as a working-class neighborhood and now abuts a more expensive area surrounding Lake Harriet.

A compact 1,050 square feet downstairs and 600 up, the stucco bungalow and two next door were built by Johnson Brothers, the first owner. So far Rueter and Dillon have converted the attic into a master bedroom and bathroom with oak flooring and millwork copied from the first floor. An Arts and Crafts–style kitchen is next on the agenda.

"Our lifestyle is oriented toward neighborhood and being outdoors," say the owners. "We know hundreds of people in Kingfield. It really is a slice of 1920s Americana, where many people care about the Arts and Crafts period and the values of living simply and well. We love and appreciate it more as time goes on."

Gardens surround this shed-roof bungalow with a gabled dormer and a brick foundation (opposite, top left). At the front is the ever-present Twin Cities sunroom. In the back is a large patio, and not far away is Lake Harriet. ▪ Although the house is small, the living room is big enough for an antique upright piano (top right). ▪ Red oak adds a deep luster to the dining room's handsome built-in buffet (bottom left). The sconces and other lighting throughout the house are original. ▪ The owners, one of whom runs an upholstery shop in a 1920s commercial building a half block away, collect antique and new greenware pottery (bottom right). ▪ Green pottery even tops the medicine cabinet in the vintage wainscoted bathroom, with its original fixtures and standard-option hexagonal white floor tile (above).

Wrapped with Soul

For a landscape architect's home, it is not surprising that the garden of this Kingfield bungalow takes a strong supporting role. Tom Kerby describes his garden as an "Asian-themed experience with emphasis on serenity and tranquility." Potted grasses and window boxes with overflowing annuals lead the eye around the corner, where a gate opens into a private world of greenery filled with shade-loving hostas and touches of color from perennials.

Serenity prevails inside as well. As soon as he saw the house, says Kerby, "I knew where the Christmas tree would go immediately!" The ledge atop the oak bookcases announcing the dining room also called out for some of the Roseville pottery collected by his partner, Cory Meyer. The handsome oak buffet, with its mullioned glass doors, is the house's signature piece. Kerby, along with family and friends, refinished all the oak woodwork in the 1,200-square-foot bungalow to give it a fresh glow. "I made a promise to the house," he recalls, "that I would restore it to what it should be, and in the process the house has wrapped its soul around my life."

Kerby's four-season porch at the front of the cream-colored stucco bungalow offers the year-round light and sun that are invaluable in Minnesota's climate (opposite, top left). Plantings pick up the rust and tan trim colors. ▪ A brick path leads to an Asian pond at the back (top right). ▪ The study's furnishings echo the rich oak tones of the window surrounds (bottom left). ▪ Although plans call for renovation of the second bathroom, this one has already been updated with new oak wainscoting and a vintage clawfoot tub salvaged from a neighbor's back yard (bottom right). ▪ Burnished to golden tones, the dining room's oak woodwork is the soul of the house (right). Linear patterns in the reproduction Arts and Crafts chandelier contrast gently with the wood's swirling grain.

As the Sears catalogue noted, "The rugged, massive cobblestone chimney adds the final touch of stability and bungalow character" (opposite, top left). ▪ Previous owners closed in both the entrance porch and the pergola on the side (top right). ▪ Bradbury and Bradbury wallpaper, added by the Jensens, encircles the dining room, running around the mirrored oak buffet and filling the plaster walls between the plate rail and the ceiling (opposite, bottom and above). The floors are maple. ▪ Beneath a box-beam ceiling, the brick fireplace in the inglenook is flanked by built-in cabinets and benches housing radiators (overleaf). Some original ceiling lights remain throughout the house.

A Step Up

I n 1917, the second year that Sears offered this six-room, one-bathroom ready-made bungalow, a Minneapolis family ordered one for itself and had it put up in the Bryn Mawr neighborhood a few miles from downtown. "The treatment of the roof, body finish, floors and walls of the interior, with a careful blending of tone from the darker brown to the light terra cotta and creams," Sears said of the "Ashmore" model (cost for materials: $1,608 to $3,632), "produces a delightful and harmonious contrast." About ten owners later—many of whom never knew or wanted to admit that their home came from a Sears catalogue—Carolyn and Tom Jensen purchased it in 1991 and now never tire of telling its story.

Once inside, visitors are drawn to the superb inglenook, raised two steps up from the living room. This medieval hideaway particularly appeals to Carolyn, who is English. The Jensens, working with Joe Metzler of SALA Architects, have made a number of improvements, notably in the kitchen, "so that it would live up to the standards of the main living rooms" with handmade tiles, honed granite countertops, and new cabinets and a breakfast nook inspired by the 3,700-square-foot bungalow's original woodwork. Plans call for an English-style guest bedroom featuring William Morris patterns and a Scandinavian Arts and Crafts renovation of the two attic bedrooms in honor of Tom's family. In the basement are an office, a bathroom, and television and laundry rooms. Off the dining room, a broad expanse of windows in the sunroom (originally the pergola) look out onto the garden, where Carolyn, a passionate gardener, has something in bloom from April to October—"a challenge in Minnesota."

The Jensens bought the bungalow to stay in their close-knit neighborhood of 1,200 households and raise their two children here. With its own downtown, a park, and views of the Minneapolis skyline, Bryn Mawr is "truly a great place to live," they say. "The woman we bought the house from was emotionally tied to this house to the point that I thought she was peculiar," adds Carolyn. "Now that I have lived here and learned to love the house, I understand how she felt."

Cozy in Como

When Richard Greene and Samuel Brungardt first stepped through the door of this 1912 bungalow near Como Park and St. Paul's Lake Como, the untouched woodwork and sense of space sold them immediately. The builders' attention to detail is apparent in the forestlike dining room, where a canopy of dark beams branches across the ceiling. Underneath, oak cabinets, posts, and wall moldings reach up from the floor to enclose stippled plaster walls wearing their original woodsy tan paint—a back-to-nature effect faithful to the Arts and Crafts movement's color sense. The bungalow has four bedrooms, two baths, and four six-by-eleven-foot closets, as well as a mudroom off the kitchen and a basement below.

The owners remodeled and restored the kitchen and baths after they moved in, upgrading the electricity and heating and adding air conditioning. With its open plan and many doors, the 1,800-square-foot bungalow lends itself to entertaining. In the two decades since they bought their bungalow from the original owners, the Marquart family, Greene and Brungardt have never found any good reason to move. "Whenever we look at another property and think about moving," they say, "those thoughts disappear after we get back home."

Nestled under a shed roof, the sun porch sits securely on the ashlar-faced stone foundation (opposite, top left). Stucco and cedar shakes on the sides add to the bungalow's woodsy feel. The sunroom windows are mirrored by a broad expanse of glass in the gabled dormer. ▪ Inside, an original Craftsman fixture lights the way up the wood-screened stairway (top right). ▪ The glass-front buffet (bottom), another original feature, houses some of the owners' collection of Red Wing and Roseville art pottery, while the plate rail provides a roost for other favorites. The dining set is a modern Stickley reproduction. ▪ In the original sanitary white bathroom, the pillbox-tank Ordway toilet dates from 1912 (above).

Built to Last

The ubiquitous Minnesota sun porch greets visitors to the St. Paul bungalow home of Mary Reichardt, who teaches English at the nearby University of St. Thomas. As a girl, she envied friends who lived in friendly bungalow communities in the Chicago area. She got her own chance to enjoy bungalow living when she moved to the Twin Cities and bought this stucco front-gabled example after it had seen at least six previous owners.

At a cost of $5,800 in 1923, the bungalow in the Hamline-Midway neighborhood was pricier than others because of the options requested by the first owners, Alvin and Julia Tavernier, including a larger kitchen with a breakfast nook and an oversized built-in oak sideboard in the dining room. "The lovely old woodwork," Reichardt notes, "needed renewing rather than complete refinishing"—a painstaking job she did on her own, thanks to skills learned as a volunteer for Habitat for Humanity. She added the leaded-glass windows with floral patterns.

"This house is rock solid and constantly inviting to homeowner and guests alike," she notes. Even a few hairline cracks in the sand-textured plaster walls and ceilings do not spell trouble, she thinks. In the basement stands the original 1920s gas canning stove, "waiting for the day I may put up a stock of preserves."

"Perhaps it's not surprising," muses Reichardt, "that the generation nurtured on cyberspace and 1980s materialism is rediscovering the simplicity, practicality, and craftsmanship of what realtors still tend to call starter homes—the implication being that you'll move up and out as soon as economically feasible." The founder of the Hamline-Midway chapter of the Twin Cities Bungalow Club, Reichardt says that "my urban neighborhood is thriving due to its diversity and interaction. It is, quite simply, an interesting place to live."

"The stucco exterior," says Mary Reichardt of her typical 1,200-square-foot midwestern bungalow, "probably will last well into this century" (above). ▪ Airtight windows and a radiator allow the porch, like many in the Twin Cities, to be used in cold weather (opposite, top left). ▪ The low attic space has been made livable, with a skylight added to supplement the two windows at the front of the two-bedroom, one-bathroom house (top right). ▪ Decorative brackets announce a subtle dividing line between the living and dining rooms (bottom). To the left of the oak buffet, a typically narrow bungalow stairway leads up to the attic.

Movie Star

Ted Madison and Diane Giovanazzi lived around the block, admiring this complex stucco-and-brick bungalow on a double corner lot in St. Paul's Phalen Heights Park neighborhood for six years before becoming the fourth owners. Built in 1921 by newlyweds, the bungalow is a typical one and one-half stories but at 2,500 square feet is larger than the norm for the Twin Cities. Its hipped and gabled roofline, originally red tiled, builds upward from the hipped entrance porch, over a taller dormered roof, and then higher still to end in a side gable. Both that roof and the dormer have medieval-looking jerkinhead (clipped) gables, a style echoed in the corbelled brick chimneys.

This attention to detail continues inside, where built-in bookshelves on either side of the brick fireplace and the dining room buffet bear floral patterns in the glass. Unlike other bungalows in the neighborhood, the main hallway features transom windows above each door. Plaster walls with oak trim rise from oak and maple floors. The kitchen was remodeled and three bedrooms added upstairs, making a total of five.

"This house is the one I've always dreamed of owning," admits Madison, who relates that the first owner, Karl "Rudy" Schmidt, was an amateur philosopher and poet. One day while walking his dog, Madison came across a verse of Schmidt's posted in a nearby poetry park: "Take or give, Life is not a mug to drain, But a Golden Cup to fill." To catch another view of the bungalow, check out *Grumpy Old Men,* filmed across the street in 1993. The house is in the background of several scenes.

A swing on the brick front porch offers a view of Lake Phalen (above). ▪ Oak French doors lead from the porch to the gray-walled music room, where the family serendipitously installed its 1920s quartersawn-oak Euphona player piano in the same place as the original owners' own piano (below left). ▪ Tuliplike flowers in spring pink and green leaded glass climb the bookcase and buffet doors (below). ▪ The fireplace mantel in the living room seamlessly continues the line of oak molding that defines the top of the adjacent built-in bookcases (opposite). The sconces are original.

In Tune with the Seasons

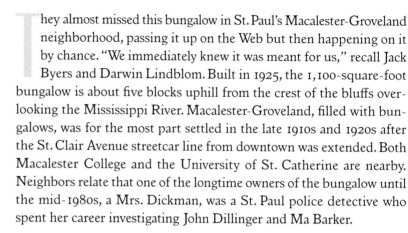

They almost missed this bungalow in St. Paul's Macalester-Groveland neighborhood, passing it up on the Web but then happening on it by chance. "We immediately knew it was meant for us," recall Jack Byers and Darwin Lindblom. Built in 1925, the 1,100-square-foot bungalow is about five blocks uphill from the crest of the bluffs overlooking the Mississippi River. Macalester-Groveland, filled with bungalows, was for the most part settled in the late 1910s and 1920s after the St. Clair Avenue streetcar line from downtown was extended. Both Macalester College and the University of St. Catherine are nearby. Neighbors relate that one of the longtime owners of the bungalow until the mid-1980s, a Mrs. Dickman, was a St. Paul police detective who spent her career investigating John Dillinger and Ma Barker.

The one-and-one-half-story stucco house sports subtle Classical Revival touches beginning with its prominent portico. Look up and an eyebrow dormer winks from the middle of the red side-gabled roof. On the east side, balancing the front portico, a small porch with windows on three sides was added in 1931, with its doorway knocked out of the dining room's original dining nook with built-in benches. "The inspiration for the white wicker decor and light blue bead-board ceiling," says Byers, "is the screened porch of my grandparents' summer cottage (a bungalow built about 1914) in Stone Harbor on the Jersey shore, where I spent many childhood vacations. This porch is a reminder of that place here in the landlocked Midwest. Our house," he adds, "is perfect for living a life in tune with the seasons. It's warm and cozy in winter and breezy and open in summer."

As new owners, Byers and Lindblom view their yard as a work in progress (top). They have already added trees and shrubs such as eastern redbud, snowball hydrangeas, and mock orange. ▪ Small in size—only 8 by 10 feet—the bungalow's porch is large in amenity (above). A light green tint was chosen to accentuate the green reflection from the Engleman ivy that covers it from June to October. ▪ Despite its classical dress outside, the three-bedroom, one-bathroom house features Craftsman details inside: a brick fireplace positioned between built-in oak bookcases as well as plaster walls, oak trim, and hardwood floors (opposite). The bath and kitchen have been redone, and plans call for a window seat to be built beneath the eyebrow dormer on the rooftop. The bungalow's attic was finished long ago, in the 1930s.

The large gabled dormer bringing light into the bedrooms upstairs adds to the authoritative sweep of the shed roof (opposite, top left). Houses on this block are offset to allow space for a garden on one side and a narrow sidewalk on the other. ▪ The broad, columned porch with a fir floor most likely was open originally but is now enclosed with distinctive multipane windows (top right). ▪ Warm southeast light stencils patterns on the furnishings and floor of the Schultzes' dining room— a symphony in oak (bottom). ▪ Although the "relatively spacious" kitchen and the bathroom had undergone minor changes, the oak woodwork, plaster walls, and oak and maple floors remained close to original condition (above).

First and Last

"This is the first house we bought, and our intention is for it to be the last, too," says Karen Schultz of the 1919 St. Paul bungalow in which she and her husband, Bob, are raising their family. The Macalester-Groveland neighborhood "feels like a small town," she adds. Residents of the neighboring bungalows and other homes built in the 1910s and 1920s walk to the grocery, hardware, pharmacy, clinic, and restaurants.

Charmed by the woodwork and built-ins—like so many others in the Twin Cities—the Schultzes bought the 1,300-square-foot bungalow when they were just two (now four make their home here). "We also liked the fact that it has three bedrooms on the same floor and that each bedroom has a very large closet," Karen explains. They set about sprucing up the exterior, substituting cedar shakes for the aluminum siding, and replaced the window trim, painting it red and the rough stucco base a neutral Arts and Crafts hue. A new garage matching the house's style took the place of one in a state of near collapse. Overgrown shrubs and a rear deck were torn out and the gardens replanted with perennials inside a handsome dry stone wall.

Working with David Herreid of Wichser and Herreid Architects, the Schultzes are renovating the basement, carving out a combined family room–bedroom, small office and workshop, bathroom, laundry room, and closets. "When this is complete, we plan to renovate the back-entry porch, adding heat and light, so that we don't have wet boots and mittens and backpacks in the kitchen." Next in line: returning the kitchen and bathroom to their period feel. Says Karen, "The bungalow's space does force us to think carefully before we bring home another new toy or object, but we feel that is a plus—we enjoy the challenge of thinking creatively about our space."

Minnesota Mission

Among the wooded streets of St. Paul's St. Anthony Park, named for the nearby falls, sits this serene one-and-one-half-story bungalow embodying Frank Lloyd Wright's precept that the "horizontal line is the line of domesticity." The brick foundation hugs the ground under a light stucco facade whose horizontality is only gently interrupted by the upward lilt of the front gable. For Ann Latvaaho and Bob Palrud, it was essentially love at first sight, with Latvaaho falling for the light-filled sunroom and Palrud for the lot and the neighborhood. "The master bedroom hooked us!" she remembers.

Over the years two bedrooms were combined into this master bedroom, but original features from oak and maple trim and built-ins to heating registers, six-over-six double-hung windows with wavy glass, and storm windows remained untouched. The new owners made adjustments, such as leveling sagging roof supports, bringing the wall sconces back to life, adding a cabinet in the stairway landing and replacing another between the upstairs bedrooms, removing linoleum hiding the kitchen's oak floor, and retiling a bathroom.

A fairly late bungalow for the Twin Cities, the house was constructed in 1924 by Andrew Presthus, his name revealed on the back of a stair tread during renovation. This and the neighboring house were built for the daughter and son of a man who owned the closest thing to a mansion in "the Park." The daughter got the "homey little box," whose present calm is belied by a checkered past: at one time Lutheran missionaries were housed here and then a loud neighborhood party giver took over.

The sunroom (opposite) brightens Minnesota winters and invites lingering in the Stickley rocker, reproduced from a Harvey Ellis design. ▪ Next to built-in glass-fronted cabinets, an efficient wood stove installed in the fireplace warms up the living room as well as the dining room behind the arched opening (above). ▪ At 2,550 square feet including the basement, this St. Anthony Park bungalow is bigger than it looks (below). It houses three bedrooms (a fourth is on the agenda), two and a half bathrooms, a basement office and pool room, and five closets, one of them a cedar closet created from a coal shed.

California Welcome

More than a thousand visitors toured this St. Paul home during a recent Twin Cities house tour, many of them no doubt surprised to find such a rugged California-style bungalow in their midst. Designed by Mark Fitzpatrick and built in 1910, the one-and-one-half-story bungalow in Merriam Park is now home to Randy and Angie Herman; they purchased it from the original family, the Lanes. A few changes were made in the original plans—the addition of radiators, closets, and a half bathroom—but the bungalow has traveled through the years with hardly a discernible change other than a reconfigured kitchen.

River rock used boldly outside for the foundation comes inside as a massive fireplace that rises in the living room from the oak floor to the beamed ceiling. Its weight is balanced by generous French doors that lead out to a glassed-in porch facing the street. Above it is a gabled screened porch designed for sleeping outside in summer's refreshing air. Throughout the house Arts and Crafts features add unusual elegance: different beamed ceilings in each room, wood paneling, plaster walls, picture rails, a buffet with leaded glass, an open staircase with perforated panels, bedrooms tucked into dormers upstairs, original bathrooms. "This house is so welcoming," say the owners. "Everyone admires its charm and warmth."

On all sides of the stucco house, the woodwork—beams, brackets, and rafter tails—is exaggerated, calling to mind the California bungalows of Greene and Greene (opposite). ▪ Arts and Crafts designers viewed fieldstones as a direct link with the earth, making them perfect symbols for the hearth at the center of most bungalows (top). ▪ The elaborate newell post uses a stylized Arts and Crafts design to represent nature, punctuated with copper centers on its trailing flowers (bottom).

Although "biffies" (bathrooms in Minneapolitan) are favorite makeover targets, the Hermans' sanitary white bathroom retains its period fixtures (above), including a ringed shower with nickel-plated mixers (left).
▪ Located above the first-floor sun porch, the upstairs sleeping porch nestles into the landscape as if it were a tree house (opposite).

THE BUNGALOW BELT

Daniel ("Make no little plans") Burnham (1846–1912) might not have been impressed by the tens of thousands of sturdy brick bungalows that have earned their place in Chicago's architectural history alongside countless landmarks of the modern movement. For little they were—in comparative size if not in aspiration or impact. Yet the 80,000 to 100,000 bungalows that circled the city between 1910 and 1940 are among the nation's most distinctive. In the number built, the uniqueness of their style, the cohesiveness of their neighborhoods, and now the commitment to preserve them, Chicago's bungalows are in a class by themselves.

Part of the story begins with the devastating fire of 1871, after which building codes encouraged brick construction. But the waves of southern and eastern European immigrant workers who flooded the city in the ensuing decades could afford little more than frame workingmen's cottages. Between 1910 and 1930, aided by the migration of southern blacks, Chicago added a million newcomers and thereby grew faster than any other American city. More prosperous oldtimers began to heed developers' calls to leave the center city.

Just as the elevator enabled Chicago skyscrapers to grow upward, streetcar lines and the "L" transported its residents outward. Rows of nearly identical brick bungalows began to girdle the city in a western crescent—a bungalow belt—creating neighborhoods from the South Shore to Norwood Park with bucolic names such as Chicago Lawn, Marquette Park, Portage Park, Galewood, Beverly, Austin, Jefferson Park, Mayfair, West Rogers Park, and the Villa. Beyond the city line bungalows changed suburbs such as Berwyn. "The move to the Bungalow Belt meant upward mobility, and in some cases flight from newer ethnic and racial groups making their way into Chicago's industrial workforce," notes Dominic A. Pacyga in *The Chicago Bungalow*.

More than public transit and aggressive marketers were at work here. At the turn of the twentieth century Chicago was the nation's mecca for

In bungalow neighborhoods such as the western suburb of Berwyn— where gables are clipped to toe the horizontal line—fences did not make good neighbors: one lawn joins another to landscape a whole community.

social and architectural progressivism. Reformers from Jane Addams at Hull House to visionaries such as Frank Lloyd Wright to the west in Oak Park preached that the way to a better soul was through a better home. Chicago itself was home to its own Arts and Crafts Society, the Prairie School, *House Beautiful* magazine, and manufacturers specializing in mass production, not to mention Montgomery Ward and Sears, which sold entire houses by mail. The siren song of modern amenities—central heat, electricity, indoor plumbing, light-filled windows, and clean air—was strong and clear as well.

Builders were ready. Although some neighborhoods were created by large developers, many builders worked on their own, buying subdivided land and either hiring an architect or using stock plans. Homeowners also might purchase a lot on their own, choose a plan they liked at the lumberyard or from a catalogue, and locate a builder or a general contractor. Developers helped secure mortgages, as did building and loan associations set up by various ethnic groups.

California Craftsman bungalows proved an inspiration for some houses built during the first blush of the city's bungalow movement, in neighborhoods such as the Villa district on the northwest side. But by about 1920 a unique bungalow form had evolved: the old workingmen's cottage wrapped in vestiges of the Prairie style. The die was cast for tens of thousands of long narrow brick bungalows shaped to fit the city's narrow lots, generally 25 to 37 feet wide by 125 feet deep. On street after street rose one-and-one-half-story homes tailored to a cold climate with a full basement, an unfinished attic, and often a garage accessed off the back alley. Unlike California bungalows that embraced the outdoors, the Windy City archetype turned inward for warmth. Their floor plans— living and dining rooms and kitchen on one side and two bedrooms and a bathroom on the other with a small hallway in between—were nonetheless open, with views flowing around corners.

Chicago bungalows may have looked about the same, but little differences in detailing helped commuters find their way home in the evening to their red or cream-colored brick bungalow: a colorful checkerboard or raised brick pattern; a front bay either octagonal, squared, or semicircular, acting as a sunroom in lieu of an open porch; limestone details that lie like Chicago snow on the brick; a low-pitched dormered hipped roof or one with jerkinhead (clipped) gables, covered in asphalt shingles

or fireproof cement tile painted red or green; a small entrance porch off to the side, secluded to keep out chills. Facades got the finer face brick, ordered from outside the city, with the backs of houses relegated to rougher common brick. As elsewhere, built-in woodwork features made the houses "artistic." For their working-class residents, the real jewels were found in the windows, where stylized nature motifs picked out in Prairie-style art glass brought Arts and Crafts ideals home to Everyman.

"Chicago bungalows are as stalwart as Chicagoans, withstanding winter after frigid winter," says Bonita Mall of the Chicago Architecture Foundation, who points to their "hunkered-down look on cold snowy days." Bungalow building came to an end with the Great Depression and World War II. As white residents moved farther out, the strict segregation that had solidified racial barriers in the city began to unravel. Blacks and then Hispanics, Asians, and Arabs joined earlier residents who had called bungalows home for a half century.

Today fully a third of Chicago's single-family homes are bungalows. To ensure their continuation as a vital foundation of urban neighborhoods, the city in 2000 launched the Historic Chicago Bungalow Initiative. This innovative education and preservation program offers owners of certified bungalows incentives to maintain them—special mortgage rates, architectural assistance, rehabilitation guidelines, seminars, and discounts on building products. To be eligible for financial incentives, bungalow alterations must meet certain guidelines. In launching the initiative, Mayor Richard M. Daley took a moment to reminisce: "For many Chicagoans, a bungalow was the first house—and the only house—they ever owned," noted Daley, who grew up in a 1939 bungalow on Chicago's southwest side built and continuously lived in by his father, the other Mayor Daley. "And for those of us who were raised in them," said his son, "bungalows will always occupy a place in our hearts."

Many working-class bungalow owners saw the world through art glass windows recalling those Frank Lloyd Wright produced for wealthier businessmen clients around the Chicago area (top). ▪ Sometimes separated by a gangway only 5 to 15 feet wide, Chicago bungalows were built so close together that neighbors bragged that they could borrow a cup of sugar through their windows (bottom left). ▪ Chicago's bungalow fever extended even to this restaurant in Oak Lawn, south of the city (bottom right).

Chicago Craftsman

Before Chicagoans moved up and out to streets of nearly identical brick bungalows, the city's working people lived in simple cottages with steep front gables. This early bungalow, built sometime between 1896 and 1906 for N. B. Marshall, can be seen as a transition from these Victorian cottages to the city's own full-fledged bungalow style, honed in the 1920s. "We have never seen a similar home," say the owners, Kathryn and Thomas Bowler.

With its cream-colored stucco trimmed in dark wood and its gabled portico outlined in stickwork, the 4,200-square-foot house (not all yet finished) in the West Ridge area on the Far North Side carries a Craftsman look promoted by Gustav Stickley and planbooks of the day. In the couple's small neighborhood of single-family homes, many of them more typical Chicago bungalows, are some other Craftsman bungalows. "But ours is older than all of these bungalows," point out the Bowlers, who are only the fourth owners. Three generations of one family, the Corcorans, lived here for sixty years.

The bungalow has a surprisingly open plan, with wide oak-trimmed openings rather than doors between rooms. Oak floors and trim in both the living and dining rooms add to the warm luster. Built-ins range from an eight-foot window seat in the living room to a dresser in the large first-floor bedroom.

Another bedroom, a bathroom, and a library also share the main floor. In the upstairs loft are the master bedroom and bath plus a nursery for the family's baby daughter. The Bowlers have repainted the bathroom in period colors and have tackled an Arts and Crafts–style renovation of the kitchen. For this they are using two built-in oak butler's pantries and glass cabinets salvaged from a period home being demolished. "The new kitchen," they say "will be a great addition to our family life."

The front porch is sheltered under the portico and the overhanging eaves (opposite, top). Two 30-foot catalpa trees frame the yard, which also has a Chinese redbud. ▪ A bracketed oak mantel tops the brick living room fireplace (opposite, bottom). Built-in bookcases on either side were removed long ago when the radiators were installed. The Bowlers added the art glass windows. ▪ Spaces flow freely in the bungalow from the living room to the dining room and into the stairhall (top). The Roycroft light fixture was originally located on the porch. ▪ In the dining room eyes are drawn immediately to the impressive oak box-beam ceiling, which appears to be holding up the high plate rail that encircles the room (bottom). The table is by Limbert, but the bungalow's original built-in buffet was sold in the 1940s.

Woodland Cottage

"Our realtor friend heard us talking about finding a cottage in the country near Lake Michigan and found this great little cottage-like bungalow with lots of natural oak woodwork, two big brick fireplaces, and lots of room to garden in a quiet neighborhood near many of our friends, and we loved it immediately," relate the owners of this 1911 bungalow, another anomaly in the West Ridge area of the Far North Side. A decade earlier than the typical Chicago bungalow, it shares little architecturally with its city neighbors but much with the models coming out of California.

Built around a red oak tree that now towers over it, the U-shaped stucco bungalow is a home that Gustav Stickley or Frank Lloyd Wright (who also designed a house around a tree in River Forest) would have commended. The post-and-beam front porch, whose exposed rafter tails form an entry arbor, has been replicated in a new deck at the back. Barrel-vaulted ceilings in the foyer and living room bid a dramatic welcome to the one-story bungalow, built originally for the Emil Hasenbalg family. The living and dining rooms are contrasts in light and dark—the former centered around flames from the hearth, the latter flooded with sunshine from casement windows on three sides.

Renovations to date, self-designed, include the kitchen, a Craftsman-style remodeling of a bedroom added in 1941, the hall, the back deck, and the basement, whose family room "now gets the most use of all." The fireplace there has been surrounded by tongue-and-groove wainscoting and Bradbury and Bradbury wallpaper. Next on the project list are the first-floor bathroom, the laundry room, the garage, and the garden shed. Say the owners, "We really enjoy living in this well-designed and efficient little house and hope to stay for a good long while."

A triple chimney punctuates the side-gabled front roof, which was originally wood shingled (top). ▪ The new porch and deck off the back frame the historic red oak with a pergola matching the one at the front entrance (above). ▪ In the living room's secluded inglenook, built-in oak benches and bookcases beg for an afternoon of reading (opposite, top left). More oak trims the windows, ceilings, and sand-textured plaster walls. ▪ The passage between the kitchen and the dining porch runs beside the red oak tree around which the house was built (top right). ▪ "The renovated kitchen is now a pleasure to use and be in," observe the owners, who have selected Arts and Crafts reproduction borders (bottom). ▪ "During the day," they say, "the dining porch is awash in wonderful light, with great views of the shady back yard and the huge oak tree growing just inches from the west wall" (overleaf). Its trim is painted birch.

Better-quality face brick was used only as far back as the house's entrance, a typical cost-saving measure (opposite, top). "Flower-boxes at the sunroom windows," Gustav Stickley suggested in 1913, "bring the garden and house into such intimate companionship that one hardly knows where one leaves off and the other begins." ▪ Set apart behind an archway, the glassed-in front bay pulls light into the living room (bottom). The brick-and-tile fireplace, between built-in bookcases, picks up the keystone motif used above the front windows. ▪ In the compact back yard, the garage's red brick walls and tiled roof tie it to the materials used for the house itself (above). Where Chicago bungalows are too narrow for a driveway, their garages are reached by a back alley.

Rhapsody in Red

Frank Lloyd Wright taught Chicago designers how to heighten a house's sense of mystery, hiding its entrance on the side, down a walkway—just like the entrance of this West Ridge bungalow. An open front porch, so useless for much of Chicago's year, has been forsaken for a modest portico on the side of the house marked by a pair of oversize planters that also owe a debt to Wright. Like thousands of others in the city's Bungalow Belt, the red brick bungalow, built in 1923, mirrors its next-door neighbor.

Yet there is nothing static about this house on the Far North Side, which is now owned by Lois Remeikis and William Gould. From the street it unfolds in layers of colors, textures, and shapes. The red brick is punched up with limestone highlights from the flower box to the window sill and keystones to the caps on the slightly battered brick piers on either side of the facade. A herringbone brick pattern framed by a soldier course adds interest from the street. The rectangular shape of the windows segues upward into a wide arch and then into the triangular pitch of the lower gabled roof, culminating in the clipped front of the uppermost tiled roof. This jerkinhead roof style, relatively rare in any other city, is one of the most distinctive features of the Chicago bungalow—whole streets of them one after another creating a unique architectural rhythm.

"The rooms flow gracefully into each other, allowing intimate dinners or large gatherings," say the owners, who have remodeled the kitchen and expanded the attic with a bedroom, dressing area, bathroom, and study. In the basement are a recreation room, sauna, wine cellar, tool room, laundry, and gardening room, together bringing the square footage to 3,500. One of the couple's favorite rooms is the breakfast nook, overlooking the back yard. "Everyone loves the warmth and openness of our home."

Artistry in Brick and Mortar

" wanted an Arts and Crafts house, and in my price range it was a bungalow or nothing," Michael Williams admits. Before he and Karen Burke found this creamy brick bungalow in the West Rogers Park area of Chicago's Far North Side, they had been looking for a while. "We wanted one that hadn't been changed or altered too much but would respond to a full restoration." A collector of Prairie School furnishings—he likes their boxy lines, rectilinear spindles, and geometric designs—Williams divulges that he loves "the thrill of finding a piece that's pretty rough and bringing it back."

That is exactly what the couple did to their new home as well, bringing it back to its as-new appearance in 1926, or even better. They refinished all the birch woodwork. "Every piece of wood in the house had been painted," he moans. And every door had been removed. Even the wire-cut face-brick fireplace had been painted, but several weeks of work got all the traces out of the tiny grooves. "The maple floors in the kitchen," he adds, "were wavy from eight layers of vinyl, tile, and linoleum."

Now the 3,700-square-foot bungalow is an exemplary tribute to early-twentieth-century Chicago design, from the basement's maple floors to the Douglas fir wainscoting in the attic and from the living room filled with Arts and Crafts treasures to the breakfast nook benches salvaged from a neighbor. One of the four bedrooms is used as a family room, and a studio takes up part of the basement.

Bungalows on the Far North Side are not as regimented as in some of Chicago's neighborhoods, and lots tend to be larger, around 35-by-125 feet. Williams, who helped locate Bungalow Belt examples for this book, marvels at how well built a Chicago bungalow is. "Essentially the entire house was made out of concrete or brick, from the basement floor to the roof," he told readers of *American Bungalow*. "They are artistry in brick and mortar."

The bungalow presents a rotund face to the street, a departure from the more typical octagonal bay front found in Chicago (below). This took more skill and thus cost more. Running above diamond-shaped insets, a limestone beltcourse underscores the semicircular shape of the front bay. ▪ Restored to its unpainted state, the brick fireplace nestles without flanking bookcases into an alcove framed by a segmental arch (opposite). The round opening acknowledges both the front bay's rotundity and Wrightian predecessors.

Generic rockers and a Morris chair snuggle into the luxurious front bay, which is wrapped with a ribbon of fine cross-patterned art glass windows (left). Wood molding at the ceiling line unites the living spaces. ▪ French doors beneath an archway signal the way toward the dining room, with the kitchen and the back door beyond (top). The Chicago artist Oscar Erickson of the Hoosier Salon made the woodblock prints. The green vase is from Ephraim Faience. ▪ The roomy attic, which covers 900 square feet, is paneled in fir (above). The first floor and the basement each occupy 1,400 square feet.

Maximum House

"Are you sure it's a bungalow?" people ask the first time they see this example on steroids overlooking Indian Boundary Park in West Rogers Park. For a 5,000-square-foot house with sixteen rooms and a two-car garage, it is a reasonable question. But oversized "bungaloid" mansions such as this, often built on corner lots reserved for them in bungalow neighborhoods, are embraced by Chicago as natural outgrowths of the city's bungalow tradition. With its ground-hugging wings and broad, sheltering roof of tile, the house is also a nod to Chicago's Prairie School legacy.

Henry J. Spanjer, a former boxer who had won gold and silver medals at the Olympics, had the two-story brick house built in 1925 and raised his family here over the next two decades. This explains the large gymnasium on the second floor, originally outfitted with a punching bag, a chin-up bar, a retractable massage table, and other workout equipment. The current owners, Philip Kraus and Dennis Northway, have turned this space into a music room.

"The previous owners, an actress and a local politician, combined the kitchen, pantry, and breakfast room into one large kitchen measuring 27 by 11 feet," explain Kraus and Northway. "They also had the living room fireplace moved to heat both the living room and the library (a former bedroom) and installed central air conditioning." For their own part, the current owners have restored the outdoor sun porch and garage, remodeled the basement, and improved the landscaping. In addition to a fruit cellar, a rustic room, and a ballroom in the basement, they have counted fifteen closets. Even though Kraus and Northway's house has nearly twice as much space as the average Chicago bungalow, they marvel that "there is no wasted space anywhere."

The lively brickwork, punctuated with limestone details, ties the house to thousands of Chicago bungalows (top). The round bay holds the dining room. ▪ Arched doorways and decorative plaster walls lend a Spanish feel to the house, not uncommon in 1920s designs (center). ▪ Billed on early plans as a playroom—perhaps to evade detection in Prohibition-era Chicago—the basement includes a wood-floored party room (bottom). Such a space was not unknown in city bungalows until liquor became legal again in 1933. ▪ The sunroom overlooks the two-car garage (opposite).

In the Villa

Not all Chicago bungalows match the archetype—the stolid brick "railroad cars" lined up cheek by jowl on narrow lots in the 1920s. In the previous decade the Arts and Crafts movement had put down strong roots in the Windy City and, allied with Prairie School designers, set out to revolutionize the American home. In the six-block Villa district on the city's northwest side, originally known as Irving Park Villa (after Washington Irving) and now a city and National Register historic district, the original developers Haentze and Wheeler mandated that all houses on its landscaped parkways be in the "bungalow mode." Among the 126 homes built largely between 1907 and 1925 were plenty of Craftsman bungalows as well as some Prairie houses and foursquares.

One of the prominent architects who helped shape the Villa was Clarence Hatzfeld, who designed several houses with half-timbered gables, including this cross-gabled corner bungalow. In addition to a number of documented Villa houses and two apartment buildings there, Hatzfeld later designed structures for city parks, including the 1929 fieldhouse at Indian Boundary Park on the Far North Side.

Begun in 1915 at a cost of $5,000, the 3,400-square-foot house skillfully ties together Craftsman forms and Prairie motifs with Tudoresque detailing. Half-timbering over the natural colored stucco in the steep gables picks up the browns of the variegated brick, which is artfully detailed in the best Chicago tradition. Surprises inside range from fine Prairie-style art glass to tile mosaics, generous built-ins, and rich wood trim outlining plaster walls whose colors are drawn from nature.

For a year in 1945–46 Chicago's famous fire commissioner Michael J. Corrigan made his home here, until he was called to assist General Douglas MacArthur in setting up a public safety plan for Japan. In 2000 *Chicago* magazine named the house, along with some Lake Forest mansions and Wright-designed landmarks, one of Chicago's thirty most beautiful homes—good company for a bungalow.

Art glass and a tile mosaic showing Dutch windmills ornament the dining room's oak sideboard (above). A rainbow of china along the high plate rail catches some of the same colors used in the tile mosaic.

Oversized brackets carry oversized eaves in the house's prominent gables, with a shed-roof dormer in between (opposite, top left). A matching garage is also on the property, which sits beside one of the Villa's 1923 stone markers. ▪ Next to a Prairie planter and an art glass sidelight, the entrance is on the side (top right). ▪ Framed by a pair of brick piers with wood capitals and four tapered wood columns, a glass-enclosed porch across the front draws in warmth (bottom).

Above the oak mantel in the living room, nature comes indoors in a scenic tile mosaic, whose serenity is continued in flanking art glass windows (left). On either side of the wire-cut brick fireplace, built-in bookcases store the owners' collection of antique cameras. ▪ In the stair hall and the living room, low slatted wood screens provide a subtle divider—there and not there, a favorite Wright device (above).

Lieber Meister

Although Louis Sullivan is not known to have ever set his hand to a bungalow (Frank Lloyd Wright designed a vacation cottage for him), the great Chicago architect's influence apparently extended up to the Villa district. There, affixed to this charming bungalow built in 1917, concrete plaques entwined with stylized nature motifs likely pay homage to Wright's *Lieber Meister,* his "dear master." A small taste of the Sullivanesque ornament found on buildings such as the Carson, Pirie, Scott department store in the Loop, the panels are just one of numerous devices used to set the red brick bungalow apart from others.

The facade is frozen music, its rooflines modulating from gabled to shed to arched roofs. Projecting and receding planes, including raised brick courses between the plaques, capture light and add soft shadows. Wood sets the tone inside the house in features such as the ceiling beams, two built-in window seats, and wainscoting in the living and dining rooms. The downstairs bedrooms have been converted into an office and a family room, while two bedrooms and bathrooms and a sitting room now fill the attic.

The owner was not looking for a house in a historic district such as the Villa. As she tells the story, "I walked in, it felt like home, and I could see its potential—especially once I remodeled the kitchen to make it a decent-size space," taking over a bedroom and a hallway. Now she calls her neighborhood "one of those stable Chicago 'islands,' a rare gem in the city that has a substantially different feel from the surrounding neighborhoods." It is the kind of close-knit community, say its residents, where children raised here return as adults to buy their own homes.

The L shape of the bungalow, which totals 3,500 square feet, is an unusual configuration given the narrow lots typical of the Chicago area (top). The entrance's broad concrete planters atop the battered concrete stair piers lend a Wrightian touch. ▪ Pairs of Sullivanesque plaques ornament the projecting planter box, underscoring architecture's close relationship to nature (center). A rosy tint was selected for the mortar to blend it into the brick tones. ▪ This built-in oak window seat in the dining room is one of a pair in the house (bottom). ▪ The unusual fireplace surround was given a faux finish before the current owner moved in (opposite).

Brown wire-cut brick was used for the facade, while less expensive common brick covers the sides (below). The stickwork in the front-facing gable sheltering the porch is paired with pebbledash stucco, which was also used for the tapered porch posts. Art glass fills the tripartite gable window. The front door is solid birch. ▪ As part of their renovation, the Harlans added an interior band of birch and maple with a stencilled frieze above (opposite). Seating alcoves and display cases for Carrie Harlan's vintage cameras now embrace a honed-slate fireplace inset with custom tiles. A tiled picture of Kentwell Cottage crowns the overmantel. The cherry settle and chair are Stickley reproductions.

Kentwell Cottage

Like thousands of Chicago bungalows, this 1914 Craftsman bungalow designed by O. J. Weymarth in the Villa district has a virtual mirror image on either side. In the case of its owners, Jerry and Carrie Notari Harlan, what they see are exceptions to the Chicago rule when it comes to bungalows. Broad where others are narrow, rustic where the typical bungalow is refined, the Harlan house—named Kentwell Cottage—says country where Chicago's norm is very much rooted in the city.

The couple liked the "solid house on an extra-wide lot on a generous boulevard" and after moving in began an interior and exterior renovation supervised by Jerry. A dormered addition at the back, simulating the pebbledash stucco found in the front gable, raised the house to two and one-half stories and converted the attic into three bedrooms, two bathrooms, and a laundry room. A breakfast room, a workroom, and a deck with a pergola were also added on the main floor, and a darkroom was created in the basement for Carrie, a photographer. Now the bungalow's original oak and maple hardwood floors stretch to 3,000 square feet.

As might be expected in their country house in the city, the Harlans look forward to "the seasonal changes centered around our cottage garden." The front berm shows off hostas and spring bulbs, while through a gate with a stained glass inset in the form of an iris awaits a back yard filled with espaliered apple and pear trees and even a raspberry patch. Within the city, they have found "that green Eden" that Gustav Stickley in 1913 prescribed for all modern homeowners.

Wedding Present

ts goal of languid horizontality cut short only by a typically narrow Chicago building lot, this 1920 bungalow in the Villa district presents a no-nonsense face to the street but smiles inside. In keeping the house in league with the ground, its architect, Theodore Steuben, may have taken a cue from local masters of the Prairie style. The broad sweep of the gabled roof, the brown brick interrupted mainly by a large quartet of windows, and a smaller recessed band marking the entrance all serve to stretch the facade as far as it will go.

Like many Twin Cities bungalows to the north, any plainness stops at the front door. Perhaps because its first owner and builder was a lumberman, the rooms were like burnished wooden vessels awaiting the arrival of the right new owners. Over the past decade Felicia and Frank Portner have filled the oak floors and oak-lined living room, mahogany-paneled dining room, and birch-trimmed sunroom with English and American Arts and Crafts furnishings and compatible pieces representing the best of early-twentieth-century design. Their large collection of Roseville pottery peeks out from various nooks and crannies.

With its generous vestibule and entrance hall, plus a center hallway leading to the bedroom and the kitchen beyond on the right side, the 2,800-square-foot bungalow, like its furnishings, is more formal than most. Yet the openness of the living-dining-sunroom space on the house's left side acknowledges changes taking place in the American home, helped to a great extent by Chicago's Prairie School pioneers.

The Portners, already bungalow owners, discovered the house while looking for a place to have their wedding—which took place here three weeks after they purchased it. "I knew it would be a perfect place to have a party, and we've had many others since," says Felicia. "I feel fortunate that so much of it is in its original form, from the hardware on all the doors and windows to the cozy bench seating in five of the eight rooms. Each time I walk in after a long day, I find I love it even more."

Right inside the typically small entrance porch awaits a warm vestibule lined with art glass (below). This turns toward a hallway lighted by the band of four small windows to the left of the door—an art glass forest to please any Prairie School devotée. ▪ With the French doors open, the dining room and the sunroom flow together as one sunlit space, although the latter has lighter birch window trim (opposite). The Tudoresque dining set pairs perfectly with medieval-looking mahogany panels that line the room.

Family Matters

In addition to its Craftsman bungalows, the Villa district has its own Chicago-style bungalows. This compact brick example dates from 1922, when Chicago's bungalow boom was well under way. Carol and Willie Cade found it on a search for a bigger house. "We were growing out of our home," says Carol, the mother of four, "and then Granddad came to live with us. This, happily, forced us to look for something larger." Expanded in the 1930s during the Great Depression to take in tenants and then again in the 1980s, the attic had been enlarged with four bedrooms and a bathroom plus dormers for light.

"With every turn I took, I thought, This will work!" Carol recalls. "It was well maintained, so we could just move in, take care of each other, and watch our children grow." They refinished the floors, put on a new roof, added central air conditioning, and restored the brick fireplace.

In addition to living spaces and the kitchen, the first floor (1,250 square feet) includes a study, a bedroom, and a breakfast room; an art room is upstairs with the other bedrooms. One of the family's favorite places to gather is around their Stickley table in the dining room. In good weather, "Everyone spills out onto the front porch's concrete stairs to sit and talk or to quietly read a book," says Carol. "It has been a wonderful home—and a great blessing." As the children leave home, bathroom, kitchen, and stairway renovations await.

A limestone beltcourse and smaller details contrast with the exterior's tan face brick, which projects in pseudo-piers at the sides (top). Above the low gabled roof over the half porch rises a gabled dormer on a hipped roof.
▪ An oak mantel deftly joins the molded-brick fireplace and its bookcases on either side (right and opposite). Prairie art glass shields the cabinets (as well as the dining room buffet) and stencils the room with stylized floral patterns from the elevated windows. A Stickley settle and chairs match the hearth's sturdiness.

Going Green

On the premise that seeing is believing, the Historic Chicago Bungalow Initiative in 2002 undertook a pilot project to restore four bungalows that had been foreclosed on and were standing vacant. Located in the Marquette Park neighborhood of Chicago Lawn on the city's southwest side, the houses were rescued to show owners and would-be owners how Chicago bungalows can be rehabilitated in ways mindful of architectural, historical, and environmental concerns. The quartet of ecologically friendly "green bungalows" met with instant success: four low- and moderate-income buyers bought themselves modernized historic homes, and thousands of other bungalow owners walked away with ideas for appropriate renovations.

Each of the four model bungalows was targeted to solve a different problem. One demonstrated how to preserve original features such as woodwork and art glass windows. The next was made handicapped accessible. The third gained an addition usable as a home office with a rear entrance, and the fourth was altered to offer a loft, cathedral ceilings, and an open plan attractive to young professionals. The rehabilitations showcased sustainable features such as energy-efficient windows, geothermal heating, low-emission paint, and recycled finishing materials. "These bungalows," said Chicago Mayor Richard M. Daley, "are wonderful examples of how to adapt beautiful historic homes to modern lifestyles in a way that retains the character while reducing energy costs and protecting the environment."

The green bungalow project was funded by Chicago's housing and environment departments, the U.S. Department of Housing and Urban Development, Southwest Home Equity Assurance Program, and Historic Chicago Bungalow Association. Scott Sonoc and Bruce Klein of Sonoc Architects designed the renovations. As Klein explained to *American Bungalow,* "We felt it would be a shame to lose a type of housing stock that is very durable and ultimately at risk of being replaced by homes that are of inferior quality and out of context with the neighborhoods."

Three of Chicago's "green bungalows" were built in 1925 by a French Canadian carpenter for $5,000 each (below). Clones with similar red brick facades, limestone details, hipped roofs, and dormers can be found citywide. ▪ This octagonal-front model is also in Marquette Park, which began as a neighborhood of Irish, German, Lithuanian, Swedish, and Polish workers and is now home to a mix of African American, Hispanic, and Arab residents (opposite, top left). ▪ Chicago bungalows' close proximity and the prevalent use of common brick at the back can be seen in the renovated bungalows (top right). ▪ One of the Historic Chicago Bungalow Initiative's goals is to encourage homeowners not to remove original features such as the art glass windows that add character to the city's modest bungalows (bottom left). ▪ In the renovation plans for three of the project bungalows, the bathrooms and kitchens were reversed to suit modern lifestyles by putting the kitchen closer to the dining room (bottom right).

Gold Coast West

like Chicago itself, the western suburb of Berwyn is known for its bungalows. The town, founded in 1890, was once home to workers at the Western Electric plant to the east in Cicero, which for decades produced America's telephones. Berwyn was settled by Polish, Czech, and other immigrants but has become more diverse over the years, gaining new residents of Mexican heritage. Even though it began as a working-class community, Berwyn—again emulating Chicago—has its own Gold Coast.

Larry and Deborah Cullen bought their imposing 1928 Chicago bungalow here because it was relatively intact and cut an hour off their commute to the city. The fact that the basement and the attic had remained unfinished especially appealed to them. "The basements of many of the bungalows we looked at were chopped up into multiple small rooms," explains Larry. "The bathroom we put in the basement is probably the extent of our basement and attic renovations." The first floor, covering about 1,800 square feet, includes three bedrooms and the original bathroom in addition to an entry, living and dining rooms, and the kitchen with its breakfast nook and pantry.

The Cullens plan a few renovations, among them replacing the kitchen cabinets with oak ones more in keeping with the house and having art glass made for all the living room windows to match the pattern above the fireplace. "We love the house and the 'hood,'" they say. "There is a great mix of neighbors, some empty nesters like ourselves, some who have lived here all their lives, others who are raising young families. Everyone gets along and looks out for each other."

The bungalow uses a Christmassy color scheme common in the Chicago area: red brick with a hipped roof of mossy green tile that seamlessly harbors a prominent front dormer (top). Snowy limestone trim caps the piers and the stairway. ▪ Six amber glass knobs remain on the doors (above). ▪ Art glass covers the pair of built-in oak bookcases surrounding the faux fireplace, which is one of the many in Chicago bungalows that are merely for show (opposite, top left). ▪ Matching the house's oak floors, an elaborate carved oak archway frames the dining room (top right). A matching oak hutch made previously for the Cullens reaches to the picture rail on the plaster wall. ▪ Windows in the light-filled breakfast nook carry through an arched motif used for other window and door surrounds (bottom left). Deborah Cullen, once the Brookfield Zoo's marketing director, fell in love with giraffes and has reminders of them throughout the house. ▪ Above an old church pew from western Kentucky in the kitchen is an oak cabinet recently fashioned by the same cabinetmaker who made the dining room hutch and the child's rocker (bottom right). The kitchen floor is maple.

Pink Flamingos, Pink Elephants

Complex intersecting roofs, which jog over the entrance porch, distinguish this large Berwyn bungalow (below). The clipped jerkinhead gable on the front is mirrored on the side, over the dining room bay. ▪ Knotty pine paneling in the "Wisconsin room" makes a congenial backdrop for the basement's log cabin–style bar, which includes a copper cooler for draft beer (opposite). Shot glasses are only one of the couple's collections, which run to flamingos, salt and pepper shakers, bedpans, model cars, and even an Elvis shrine—appropriately, "lots of 50s stuff!" says Douglas Faulds.

Prohibition, mandated by the Eighteenth Amendment (1919) to the U.S. Constitution to begin in 1920, happened to coincide with the start of Chicago's bungalow boom. Forbidden from publicly consuming alcohol, a number of local bungalow owners apparently went underground, building party rooms in their commodious bungalow basements to imbibe out of sight of prying eyes. The bar in the basement of Douglas and Roxanna Faulds's Berwyn bungalow gives every appearance of being a 1950s addition—and the house itself, built in 1935, came two years after Prohibition's repeal—but it continues a time-honored Chicago tradition. The bar remains one of their favorite rooms.

A twin one foot narrower than its next-door neighbor, the large tan brick bungalow was built by two brothers who put up several others on the street. One was an architect, the other a contractor, and this was his house. They placed the pair on three lots but ran out of room when it came time to put in the two driveways between the houses. The contractor got a larger garage, complete with heat, water, and space for two and a half cars.

The brothers paid great attention to details. Face brick was used on the sides as well as the front of the bungalow because both are so visible. A brick beltcourse travels above the windows, turning corners to highlight the bungalow's complex form. The gutters are copper. Inside top-of-the-line features from hardwood floors to plaster walls, crown molding, and art glass raise the house out of the ordinary. Expanding the ground floor's 1,600 square feet, the owners finished the attic with a master bedroom, bathroom, dressing area, and skylights not visible from the street. Previous owners who were ballroom dancers practiced their steps in the mirrored rec room in the basement. "This was the first house we looked at," they say. "It was love at first sight."

Prairie Autumn

I f it had a wide front porch, this double-gabled stucco house from 1916 in suburban River Forest might be any bungalow, anywhere. But because it was built in the frequently frigid Midwest, a porch was sacrificed in favor of a sunroom that has now been annexed to the living room. The oak-paneled entry hall, on the side of the house, also acknowledges Chicago winters—it is contained several steps below the raised living areas and the front bedroom, much like Frank Lloyd Wright's Tomek House (1906) in Riverside to the south. River Forest in fact is Wright Country, next door to Oak Park and home to numerous Prairie School landmarks.

For three decades this tidy one-and-one-half-story bungalow has been owned by Jane Browne, who grew up just four blocks away and bought it so her daughters could attend the same schools as she had. It has since been filled with a robust gathering of Arts and Crafts and Prairie furnishings as warm as the mica lampshades that "shimmer like a gathering of summer fireflies," she says. Browne, who works in an Arts and Crafts antiques business, is perfectly positioned to find suitable pieces as well as contemporary craftspeople to fashion custom fittings and furnishings. In the dining room a quartersawn oak plate rail, vertical trim, and ceiling beams were added to create a forestlike space. Other custom-made additions have included a spindled screen to open up the stairway to the attic, eight skylights, and a recreated tin ceiling in the kitchen.

Browne and Celeste Rue, a classical pianist, have also converted one of the first floor's two original bedrooms into a music room. Adjacent to it is a whimsical bathroom dedicated to Theodore Roosevelt that retains its original hexagonal tiles, pedestal sink, toilet, and oak medicine cabinet. The upstairs includes a master bedroom and a new bathroom created from one bedroom, plus a guest room and an open den. "My younger daughter reminds us on a weekly basis that she would love to trade homes so she could rear her family here," Browne says. "If we ever left, it would stay in the family. Others may want a mega mansion, but give us our garden and simple bungalow life."

With their returned eaves adding a striking note, the steeply pitched gabled roofs bring to mind English Arts and Crafts antecedents (above). The effect is strengthened by the English cottage garden. The one-car attached garage is all original. ▪ The house's public rooms flow freely from living room to dining room and kitchen beyond (opposite). Greens, reds, and golds—the colors of the prairie in autumn—infuse the bungalow with a natural warmth. The dining chairs came from Fore Johnson, part of the Stickley furniture line, and the bowls are English Arts and Crafts.

THE NATION'S CAPITAL

Beyond the marble monuments, past the soldierly lines of row houses, the nation's capital is a city of bungalows, ringed by suburbs filled with even more of them. By the mid-1910s Washington, to borrow a phrase from Burgess Johnson's "Bungal-Ode" of 1911, could be described as "east bungalongitude": Bungalows were beginning to catch on in the city's outer reaches, from Brookland in the northeast, to Takoma on the northern boundary, to Chevy Chase and later American University Park in the northwest. Over the state line in Maryland, Hyattsville, Mount Rainier, Rockville, Silver Spring, and especially Takoma Park made the bungalow their own symbol of progressive living. Across the Potomac River in Virginia, bungalows soon covered lots in suburban developments launched in Arlington and Alexandria. Never in the architectural avant garde, the capital was happy to follow the national passion for bungalows.

Bungalows arrived for many of the same reasons they were adopted elsewhere. From about 1873 through the 1890s, first railroad lines and then electric trolleys began to open up the countryside for new suburban homes. Fortunate city residents—even presidents—had been in the habit of fleeing to "the heights" to escape the malarial pestilences rising from the marshy Potomac River south of the White House. With federal employment tripled by the 1880s to about twenty-three thousand, and a number of federal agencies moving away from the monumental core, real estate sales boomed. All those government bureaucrats had to live somewhere, and a clerk's modest yearly salary of about $1,000 might stretch pretty far in a builder's bungalow or one from Sears. Pitches to come out where the water was clean and the air healthful found ready listeners even without enticements such as tree-lined streets, electricity, sewers, and all the other conveniences of modern life.

Washington's first commuter suburb, one particularly bungalow rich, was founded on the Maryland-District boundary in 1883 and expanded over the next decade by Benjamin Franklin Gilbert. He called it Takoma, an Indian name meaning "high up, near heaven." Even

Takoma, one of the capital's historic in-town commuter suburbs, is lined with streets of modest bungalows much like these on Whittier Place.

Designed by Milton Dana Morrill, a former federal architect, and completed in 1909, the trolley station in Alexandria's Rosemont community was said to be "a station that any suburb of New York would be proud of."

Clara Barton weighed in on the location's salubrious benefits, which included springs with fresh drinking water. Gilbert's vision of a progressive community, one maintained to this day, encompassed resort hotels, a sanitarium, and country houses whose residents would practice civic activism. Takoma's lifeline was the B&O Railroad until electric streetcars began to roll in 1893, three years following Takoma Park's incorporation; Gilbert became its first mayor. Not long after Washington's first branch library was opened in Takoma in 1911, bungalows began to join its picturesque Shingle, Stick, and Queen Anne–style houses and simple Victorian cottages. These modest homes, some of them ready-to-assemble kits shipped on the nearby rail tracks, fulfilled Gilbert's goal of reaching out to people on a government employee's budget. "All you need is a moderate income," noted a brochure. The influx of federal workers during World War I helped make bungalows the housing of choice here and throughout the metropolitan area.

The new public transportation that enabled residents of a somewhat integrated city to move farther out ended up segregating Washington more along racial and income lines. But in city neighborhoods as diverse as middle-class Brookland and tonier Chevy Chase, bungalows found their place. Like Takoma Park, Brookland depended on the B&O. Government scientists, immigrants, and African Americans settled into its bungalows and eclectic houses after 1887. Beginning in 1890 two Nevada senators plotted out Chevy Chase, which extends from the city's northwestern boundary into Montgomery County, Maryland. The streetcar line they laid on Connecticut Avenue got residents downtown in thirty-five minutes. Advertisements noted that people "of moderate means make their homes here." They were the ones who built bungalows amidst the grander turn-of-the-century styles.

Colonial Virginia was not immune to the bungalow's charms. In Arlington (named for Robert E. Lee's mansion), bungalows came to dominate the housing stock. From 1790 to 1847 the area had been included in the ten-mile-square district set aside for the federal capital. By the late 1890s city residents could take the trolley out to still-rural Cherrydale, established in 1893, but by 1900 it was said that the

"demand for houses by tenants far exceeds the supply." Arlington's greatest growth spurt came between 1920 and 1939, when bungalows (comparatively narrow because of Arlington's narrow lots) were second in popularity only to Colonial Revival homes. The miles of tracks that made Washington a transportation hub also brought mail-order bungalows to Arlington and the rest of the region after World War I.

The development of the American city from colonial-era port to streetcar suburb can be seen in nearby Alexandria (named for John Alexander, an early landowner). Just west of Old Town, Rosemont's streets were laid out on former farmland beginning in 1908 in typical streetcar-suburb fashion: short blocks facing the trolley station and long perpendicular blocks to shorten commuters' walks. Both the trolley and the train—and later Metrorail—made it "Washington's most accessible suburb." The developer's ads promised "all the conveniences and improvements of the city ... without having to live there." At $4,000 to $5,000, the first houses, many of them bungalows, were large and comfortable. Today the heritage of Rosemont and a number of the region's other bungalow neighborhoods—among them Takoma and Takoma Park, Chevy Chase, Rockville, and Arlington—have been recognized as local, state, and national historic districts, designated as landmarks along with the capital's marble monuments.

Washington is a famously cosmopolitan place, a cultural melting pot that flavored bungalow choices here as well. But just as the capital's planners turned to classical sources for the buildings that line the Mall, Washington's bungalow builders for the most part took an equally conservative path. The typical Washington bungalow, fittingly, is the American archetype of a bungalow: a side-gabled, one-and-one-half-story structure with a central dormer (capped by a gabled or shed roof), and a columned porch nestled under the front overhang, all on a solid masonry foundation holding a basement, erected by a builder using a planbook. Metrorail may have replaced the railroad and trolley lines that first got Washington residents and bungalows together, but a handsome restored bungalow in the area today remains *almost* as coveted an address as 1600 Pennsylvania Avenue.

Bungalows spread eastward to Prince George's County in Maryland. As a child the author lived in Hyattsville in this side-gabled bungalow resembling thousands of others in the Washington area (bottom left and right).

Reinforcing the horizontal symmetry of the 4,000-square-foot house, a pair of gabled porches flank the entry and a smaller gabled dormer (opposite, top left). The bungalow's ashlar gray granite was used also for the central fireplace. ▪ Framed by paired columns holding shallow arches, the inglenook (top right) is the bungalow's central architectural symbol—uniting outside and in. ▪ Diners have a view of a verdant deck and arbor (bottom). Tall-back Wrightian dining chairs and Edward Curtis photographs subtly set an Arts and Crafts tone. ▪ New pocket doors lead from the living room to the library (above). ▪ Separating the dining and living rooms, a Mackintosh-style rug defines the entrance hall and directs the traffic flow to the back (overleaf).

Butterfly Bungalow

By 1916, when a promotional brochure for Chevy Chase opined that "each home here would bear a touch of the individuality of the owner, where each home would possess an added value by virtue of the beauty and charm of the surrounding homes," the new suburb's Washington section was almost sold out. There was room for one more, however: this imposing double-gabled bungalow designed by William Randolph Talbott and finished—a prophecy quickly fulfilled—the same year for $5,500. Talbott soon left to serve in World War I but later became a highly regarded government architect, designing veterans hospitals for two decades. The builder and first owner, Walter C. Brashears, sold the house after just one year.

For the past decade it has been the domain of Thomas Hier and William Myhre, who have honed it to museum elegance. The massive stone hearth in the baronial entrance hall drew them in, and they were sold, particularly because of the house's generous public spaces. Working with the architect Kevin Kim and Peterson and Collins builders, the owners then set out to correct more than a half century's changes. A living room wall blocking the view of the hall was torn out and replaced with rectilinear columns. Painted woodwork was stripped and new cherry wainscoting added to enrich the living room and library. The kitchen was remodeled to suit family gatherings around the cook, complete with a second fireplace to warm a new breakfast area overlooking the landscaped rear terrace. "The house is grand in a way and yet very intimate," suggests Hier, "perhaps because of the quality of the materials and the warmth of the wood."

Upstairs, an addition not visible from the street raised the roof and inserted a master suite and a large home office into a pair of gables recalling the ones so prominent on the bungalow's facade; a guest room snuggles into the front dormer. "This house is definitely more than just a house for us," adds Hier. "It has become the embodiment of a way of life—a warm, welcoming environment to share with friends and family. It's very likely that we will be in this house until the ends of our lives."

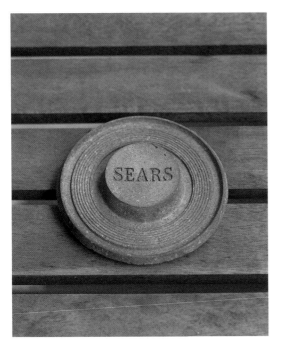

"Neither Extreme Nor Extravagant"

When a realtor showed Nancy Malan this bungalow in American University Park, she liked it immediately because it was so similar to the apartment in which she had been living. The openness, the high ceilings, the old-fashioned aspect all appealed to her. "It was a match as soon as I walked in. It just felt right," she says. Once farmland on the city's northwestern edge, the property was eventually owned by the Methodist Church, which has a seminary nearby. Bungalows made accommodating one-story retirement homes for its clergy in the 1930s. Once the land was sold to developers, center-hall colonials popular in the 1940s mixed in along streets filled with simple bungalows.

Only after Malan had moved in did a friend ask, "Do you know that this is a Sears house?" He pointed to the "Osborn" model in *Houses by Mail: A Guide to Houses from Sears, Roebuck and Company.* There it was, altered somewhat, but the measurements were an exact fit. "While the Osborn is neither extreme nor extravagant," reported the Sears catalogue, "it has all the earmarks of a cozy, well-planned, artistic home." Offered from 1916 to 1929, the house cost between $1,163 and $2,753 before labor.

Malan's one-and-one-half-story "Osborn," ordered in 1919 by Eugene and Louise Blackford, has two bedrooms and one bathroom reached by a short hall alongside the dining room. Three porches—at the entry (now closed in) and off the dining room and the back bedroom—extend the house into nature. Pine floors and the original woodwork remain, but doors between the living and dining rooms were missing. In addition to laboriously removing paint from all the woodwork, Malan has added French doors to close off drafts on the front sun porch. Although the common rooms "are big enough for a family, this is a good one-person house," she observes. "I feel like I'm just where I belong."

Under its gabled roofs, this Sears "Osborn" is a sophisticated melding of stucco, shingles, and wood trim (top). The terra-cotta color scheme, trimmed in muted blues and gray, emphasizes the bungalow's horizontality. ▪ A Sears plaque was saved from a prior owner's fence (center). ▪ The cabinets (bottom) were found stored in the basement. According to the floor plan in the Sears catalogue, they probably were originally built into the dining room. ▪ Malan added the Gothic mirror above the fireplace just inside the front door (opposite). Another fireplace is in the basement.

Sky High

One of a quartet of bungalows in a row in American University Park, this 1939 latecomer reaches sky high. Not only does it sit regally on an elevated corner lot, it has also been remodeled inside to take advantage of the house's full height. An earlier owner who was an architect removed the ceiling over the living-dining area and added skylights to open up the 2,500-square-foot bungalow. When Albert Ruesga and William Niedzwiecki moved in recently, they took out a spiral stairway leading to the second floor, filling in the mezzanine to match the existing railing. Stairs near the kitchen at the back of the house now provide access to the skylighted master bedroom upstairs.

Except for its oversized gabled dormer, the side-gabled house would be the prototypical Washington-area bungalow. Ruesga, who had been living in a Dupont Circle condominium, was first struck by the porch and then the light-filled spaces inside. "Desperate for some green space," he began to dream of sitting on the broad front porch, sipping a mint julep. "The house looked like it was surrounded by a tiny urban forest," encompassing maples, eastern red cedars, dogwoods, and azaleas. In addition to the bedroom and bathroom upstairs, a full basement dug out by the previous owner includes three bedrooms, a bathroom, and a laundry room. Ruesga and Niedzwiecki added wood floors here and on the second floor.

In the spacious yard they planted twenty trees, including magnolias, a cherry tree, a hemlock, two cryptomerias, and Leland cypresses for privacy. "We love the finches and nuthatches that visit the bird feeder just outside our kitchen," Ruesga says, noting that the kitchen is next on the renovation list. But in all the work, one thing was overlooked. "We were so busy fixing up the house after we moved in that we forgot to sit on our front porch in the summer and try those mint juleps!"

Recognizing the house's birthright in the Moderne 1930s, deep salmon-colored steps segue into the softer salmon hue of the siding, trimmed in crisp white (above). ▪ Classical columns appropriate to the nation's capital lend dignity to the front porch, which has a bead-board ceiling and a copper roof (opposite, top). ▪ The living room, now an atrium open to a cathedral ceiling, fills with light even on rainy days (bottom left). The 1940s Heywood-Wakefield cabinet holds a family Art Deco tea set, a model of Angor Wat, and a papier-mâché head used in parades. On the ledge is a Thai Buddha. ▪ With the former dining room converted into part of the living area, the back bedroom on the first floor was turned into a secluded dining room overlooking the deck and back yard (right). Another bedroom is a study.

California Dreamin'

By 1910, when this imposing Craftsman bungalow was built, the two-year-old Rosemont development in Alexandria, Virginia, numbered about six homes. "Dwellings are springing up as if by magic," exclaimed a local newspaper. If not for the trolley that put downtown Washington just five cents and eighteen minutes away, the area would have been considered unthinkably rural. Thomas Hulfish, owner of an Alexandria hardware store, took a gamble on the new streetcar suburb. His wife, a voice teacher, is said to have chosen the design from a magazine in 1908—apparently one promoting California bungalows.

The free-flowing interior today recognizes three decades of ownership by the Carlson family, including Jane, a teacher, and S. Lee Carlson, AIA, a government architect. On the first floor they created a circular layout, opening up the back of the house with a family room in a sunny atrium adjacent to the kitchen. In between, broad steps rise comfortably to the second floor, where six rooms were carved out of the attic space. Altogether the house now stretches to 2,700 square feet plus another 1,370 in the basement.

"Our children's friends immediately felt the openness and gave in to their urge to discover—and run through the house!" recalls Jane. The bungalow had been one of Rosemont's first gathering places, where neighbors came to hear the new wireless radio. The three Carlson children followed suit, inviting friends over to warm up on the old radiators after sledding on nearby Shooter's Hill in the shadow of the Egyptian Revival–style Masonic Memorial (1932), to learn ice hockey on the front porch, or to retreat in summer to the shade of the Osage orange trees in the yard. "We were drawn in by the house's simple charm and potential for growth," says Jane, who looks back fondly at the welcoming home the bungalow has offered "in a genuine neighborhood," just as the developers of Rosemont planned a century ago.

On the brick porch, tapered columns support the broad roof, which has a bead-board ceiling (below). Hulfish Hardware Store in Old Town supplied treasured features such as an unusual bronze door ring that turns for entry, ordered from Gustav Stickley's line. ▪ Windows in the house's shed dormer open onto the master bedroom on the second floor, one of three upstairs bedrooms (opposite). Elevated on its pedestal-like berm, the elegant bungalow is widely regarded as Rosemont's finest.

A carefully placed mirror above the living room mantel felicitously multiplies the bungalow's diamond-paned windows (left). Light fixtures here and in the dining room came from Stickley, as did a cabinet moved to the basement. A wall to the left was closed off to hide a view into the bathroom and one of the two downstairs bedrooms. ▪ Transoms over the tall windows facing the front porch increase the light flooding into the dining room (above). Walls and ceilings are horsehair plaster. Yellow pine was used for the floors, oak for trim such as the dining room plate rail. Beamed ceilings mark the living areas.

Almost Perfect

The owners of this cheerful double-gabled bungalow in Alexandria's Rosemont did not set out to buy a bungalow. The wife, interested in the Scottish designer Charles Rennie Mackintosh (1868–1928), wanted something from the early twentieth century. "This is almost perfect," she told her husband when she saw the 1913 house. Shortly after moving in, they decided to remove interior shutters covering the expansive living-room windows. "In the process, paint on the window trim chipped, revealing chestnut wood beneath," she recounts. "Thus began the renovations that are still ongoing." White paint covering the white and red oak, ash, and chestnut trim was stripped, the all-white color scheme outside was changed to earth tones, asbestos shingles were replaced with cedar, and the yard was landscaped and the driveway bricked over. Doors found in the basement were canabalized for molding. Kitchen and bathroom renovations await.

Hidden away at the back, on the site of the former porch, the well-traveled owners have left their own mark: an extraordinarily refined family-room addition, designed by Jim Viviano, that celebrates contemporary craftsmanship while being faithful to the house's Arts and Crafts heritage. Built-in cabinets of ash, punctuated by a breakfast nook, ring the room, all meticulously crafted by Jon Haberman and overseen by the contractor John Nugent.

"I'm stuck in the beginning of the twentieth century!" exclaims the owner, who has given up Danish modern furnishings in favor of Stickley et al. "If those are antiques, I'm for them," she says.

The 2,000-square-foot bungalow has snapped back to life with its new coat of paint (opposite, top left). The entrance is on the side, through the screened porch. Four prominent gabled dormers light the bedrooms upstairs. Medieval-looking monk's heads guard the porch light fixture. ▪ In the living room (top right) Arts and Crafts furnishings and elaborate woodwork, including a picture rail and ceiling trim, carry on a conversation. Gustav Stickley produced the settle and the ladder-back caned chair at left, grouped with a distant chair by Lifetime. Between the windows is a tall Limbert desk; the tall side table is by Michigan. Turkish carpets throughout the house were purchased during the owners' stay in Izmir. ▪ The dining room's wainscoted plate rails hold blue ware from American blue willow to Villeroy and Boch and Royal Copenhagen's Tranquebar (bottom). An Art Deco sideboard coexists with the L. & J. G. Stickley dining table and the Limbert chairs and buffet at right. A card found in the woodwork identified Hugh E. Cason as the carpenter. The chandelier is antique, while the table lamp is a modern Arts and Crafts interpretation.

Beneath a cathedral ceiling of fir with recessed lighting, broad expanses of windows invite light into the new great room (left). The television is hidden behind a cabinet at left finished with delicate ebony and maple insets. Planters in the Weller Forest pattern bring nature into the window-ringed room. The chandeliers are reproductions from Buffalo Studios.
▪ In the husband's glass collection are ethereal Art Deco vases by Gallé and Daum (above).

Good Bones

In 1909 adventurous homeowners were enticed out to Rosemont with advertisements promising "absolutely every advantage you can get in the center of town with added advantages of green lawns, pure air, [a] fine view and big lots at less than one-third city prices." By 1917 the W. H. Wright family had moved into this new $3,350 bungalow less than a block from the trolley station. It was one of five variously styled bungalows constructed before World War I by John Smithdeal, a Baltimore builder-designer.

For nearly two decades it has been the home of the Manstofs: Jane, a special events coordinator for the Torpedo Factory art cooperative on Alexandria's Potomac River waterfront; Alan, who formerly owned the popular Chesapeake Bagel Company; and their two children, Eric and Kate. "The house had good bones," says Jane, "but I was appalled at how it had been renovated." The front porch had been closed in and the dining room and den ceilings lowered to create more headroom upstairs, but worse was the attic expansion that jeopardized the bungalow's structural stability. After a year of planning, the family moved out for nearly another year to avoid the rehabilitation work and construction of an addition that nearly doubled the bungalow's size to 3,600 square feet.

Bob Lewis of Lewis and Holt designed a large family room at the back to replace a small porch, the upstairs was corrected and modified to hold a master suite and three other spacious bedrooms with built-ins, and the basement has been finished with an office, a bathroom, a kitchen, and a laundry room. A period-style kitchen now stands at the center of the enlarged house, mediating between old and new.

"Our realtor felt that the house was less than ideal because it did not have a central hallway," recalls Jane, an avid antiques collector. "That has come to be the thing I love best—the way each room opens up into another." When the Manstofs read the Sunday papers in the front solarium, they can see into the living room, the dining room, and all the way to the back yard. "I think of our house," she adds, "like a marriage: you tend to ignore faults, instead choosing to appreciate its best qualities." Alan, who saw the bungalow's potential when they purchased it, enjoyed the challenge so much that he has moved on to renovating other local historic buildings.

Under a hipped roof, striped awnings shade the front porch, which is enclosed with six-over-six windows (top). The bungalow was reshingled with cedar shingles and stained a slate gray. ▪ Bonnie, the family's border collie, has her own doggie bungalow in the yard (above). ▪ The solarium-porch leads into the original living room, which has a brick fireplace (opposite).

An earlier owner expanded the living room by taking over one of the two downstairs bedrooms (left). The second bedroom beyond the piano has been converted into a den.
▪ The new family room at the back uses multi-pane windows to relate it to the glassed-in front porch (below). The sculpture at far left is by Alan Manstof. ▪ Bead board and an exaggerated stairway bracket, which mimics the original roof rafter tails, tie the new parts of the house to the old (opposite). At the top of the stairs is Jane Manstof's cozy study; bedrooms and bathrooms are to the left and right. The original bathroom is below the stairs.

A Keeper

I t would be natural to assume that the former keeper of the National Register of Historic Places might live in a rambling Victorian mansion or a landmarked Federal townhouse in the heart of the capital. The truth is that William J. Murtagh, the first keeper of the National Register following passage of the National Historic Preservation Act of 1966, lives in an unusual bungalow on one of the oldest streets in Alexandria's Rosemont. One of only three documented hollow-tile houses in this historic district (others are found in a later subdivision), it was built in 1916 for about $3,250 by the builder-designer John Smithdeal. After moving to the bungalow from Old Town more than two decades ago, Murtagh uncovered the model for his home in a 1913 issue of *Bungalow Magazine.*

As interesting as the oversized "Metro" hollow-tile exterior, coated with slag to roughen the finish, are the panels in the box-beam ceilings covering the living area; they are made of one-inch-thick pebbledash (concrete mixed with small stones). Several of the heavy panels in the former dining room fell and had to be rebuilt. One of the two bedrooms has now been converted into a classically furnished dining room filled with family heirlooms, as is the entire house. Plants fill a sunny greenhouse added off the kitchen at the back.

Murtagh bought the house (from an architectural historian colleague) not because it was a bungalow but because it was close to a planned Metrorail stop in Alexandria. It was the trolley that brought Rosemont's first homeowners—and the modern subway that helps keep residents here today. The bungalow, says the former keeper, "is just the best type of house to live in, especially as you get older. It's like an apartment with a garden."

Decorative brackets and a cross-gabled roof (originally metal) with wide-shingled gables enliven the exterior (below). William Murtagh restored the porch, removing inappropriate twisted-metal railings added earlier. Occasional tenants find the basement cozy. ▪ The Alexandria historian William Seale has suggested that the river-rock fireplace may have been built with pavers taken up from Alexandria's historic streets (opposite). The 1905 Conover piano was bought for Murtagh by his parents when he was a teenager. Its lamps were inherited from an aunt. Although Murtagh calls the portrait "Uncle George," the subject is no relation.

Arlington Archetype

Most traces of the cherry orchards for which the Cherrydale neighborhood of Arlington, Virginia, was named in 1893 have just about vanished from this close-in suburb a few miles from the capital. But farmhouses mixed in with its Queen Annes, foursquares, and omnipresent bungalows, as well as a few cherry trees along Quincy Street (formerly Cherry Valley Road), vividly illustrate the area's rich past as farmland whose produce was sold in Georgetown markets across the Potomac River. By 1914 more than two hundred houses had sprouted up on Cherrydale's 311 acres, spurred over the previous decade by railroad and trolley lines that gave commuters a short ride into the city.

The previous year a subdivision named Robert B. Harrison's Dominion Heights had been dedicated, and on one of the Harrison family lots adjacent to some of Cherrydale's remaining orchards this frame bungalow was built about 1923–24. It was sold to a lawyer in 1924 for $8,500. When Tracey Fisch first saw it more than seven decades later, an addition off a remodeled kitchen had made the house roomier, but the remainder of the orchards had been sold off for neighboring houses in 1978. Fresh from the Boston area, "I wanted an old house like I had seen in Massachusetts," she admits. "There are two types of people—those who want character and those who want something new." Now she and her husband, Clinton, who develops historic buildings, have the best of the old and the new.

From the modernized kitchen with its tile counters and period-style cabinets she can watch her two young daughters play in the airy addition, whose bead-board wainscoting and buttery walls fit seamlessly into the old bungalow. The fireplace here is the second in the house. A Dutch door leads down to a comfortable family room in the finished basement. Two bedrooms and a bathroom are tucked into the gabled roof, while another bedroom and bath are on the first floor, which, says Tracey, "may squeak in places, but we just get used to it."

Distinctive rectangular brackets selected for the sweeping gabled roof appear on others along the same street (above). Four short tapered posts carry the porch across the front of the house and under aged oak trees that attracted the owners. ▪ In the sunny addition that extends the kitchen into the back yard, a sturdy riverstone hearth, bead-board molding, and classical window surrounds tie together new and old (below). ▪ For the dining room, located in a wide bay, the previous owner selected a cheery cherry red—an appropriate reflection of Cherrydale's history (opposite).

A Bungalow for Two

Arlington was still ripe for development in the early 1920s, when it saw one of its greatest eras of growth. By 1924 the local telephone directory included a listing for this romantic yellow bungalow in Cherrydale—a straggler in A. J. Downing's nineteenth-century campaign to spread country cottages on landscaped grounds throughout the nation. It may have been a weekend retreat reached on the nearby trolley line. No doubt its owners enjoyed the neighborhood's rural character but welcomed the coming of modern improvements such as a plumbing code, testing of well water, and a new water and sewer system.

Now owned by Christopher and Elizabeth Richard, the corner bungalow on a double lot captures the coziness long conjured up by the very term *bungalow*—a love nest, a "bungalow for two," as a popular song later rhapsodized. Just back from living overseas, the Richards "wanted a little character, a little history, convenient to Washington" and found it here, complete with ceilings tall enough for Chris.

An architect who previously owned the 1,600-square-foot house built a sunroom addition off the kitchen at the back with a den, a bedroom, and a bathroom, for a total of three bedrooms and two baths. Little else, including the woodwork, had changed much over the years. In the back yard are a pond and a tool house. Despite a lack of closets for storing treasures collected during their world travels, "It was love at first sight," recalls Elizabeth. So who said that Washington has no sense of romance?

The hipped roof jogs at the front to shelter the porch beneath its eaves (top). At the rear is the breakfast room added adjacent to the kitchen. Doric porch columns contrast with the rugged stone porch foundation, while green sawn-wood rafters add to the bungalow's cottage charm.
▪ A fireplace inset with large boulders beckons as soon as the front door is opened (bottom). Located in the dining room rather than the living room, it may have been designed for casual weekend meals around the fire. ▪ Below diamond-paned windows, a wood-paneled built-in seat fills the dining room bay (opposite). The owners, like many Washingtonians, are world travelers and have been posted abroad in Singapore and Italy.

Remodeler's Delight

For someone who remodels old houses for a living because "new homes don't have any character," this 1913 cottage-style frame bungalow in Rockville, Maryland, has been a dream come true for Mark Goldsborough. His wife, Nikki, first suggested buying an old urban house so they could move away from suburban subdivision living and walk to stores or a movie downtown. "Now we can't think of a place we'd rather be," they say.

Long the rural seat of Montgomery County, Rockville was pulled closer to the capital by its new railroad tracks in 1873 and electric streetcar lines at the turn of the century. Soon its hotels and boarding houses offered weekend and summer refuge for city residents. By 1926 even the mayor lived in one of the town's growing list of bungalows. The Goldsboroughs' home was one of the earliest, built the year after the Chautauqua and silent films first came to town.

The house's broad veranda and hipped roof beneath a canopy of aged trees give it the air of a compact southern mansion. Dr. Washington Waters and his wife, Elizabeth, had the local designer-builder Franklin H. Karn construct it on land next to Elizabeth's family property. Within two years new owners had turned it into their summer escape. For a half century beginning in 1944, the house was known as the Wootton bungalow when descendants of one of Montgomery County's pioneer families lived here. The next owner began the laborious process of restoring the bungalow, work the Goldsboroughs are patiently completing.

From its ten-foot-tall foyer encircled by French doors holding 360 original panes of glass to its mezzanine-ringed atrium punctuated by a two-story, Eastlake-style brick fireplace, this is no ordinary bungalow. At the apex of the pyramidal roof a skylight pours light into the 3,200-square-foot house, which is located in a historic district. Off the entrance hall, behind their glass screens, are formal living and dining rooms; beyond are a family room anchored by the great hearth, two bedrooms and a bathroom, and the kitchen. Upstairs are two bedrooms, a sitting room, and two baths. When the kitchen is remodeled, the back porch restored, a tall bouquet arranged on a Limbert table no. 146 in the foyer, and a swing readied on the restored front veranda, the Goldsboroughs will look back on a job well done.

Hipped dormers with flared eaves usher light into the upper story, while mitered bays on the sides turn the living areas into sunrooms (opposite, top left). The shutters have been restored so that they all now work. ▪ "When we saw the foyer we were sold on the house," say the Goldsboroughs, who have refinished the maple floors (bottom left). ▪ Albert and Josephine Wootton covered the atrium with a ceiling, confining the fireplace to its own room (right). Sherry and Joe Tomley later reopened it and also added the upstairs bedrooms.

Homegrown

Dale Stewart, an architect, is a modernist, while his wife, Sallie, a landscape designer, prefers colonial architecture. "So we met in the middle," says Dale about the house he designed for his family in Silver Spring, Maryland, not far from Sligo Creek. Their award-winning home, completed in 2001, combines a bungalow's scale with the attention to detail found in Greene and Greene's "ultimate bungalows"—plus enough historical references to please Sallie and sufficient flowing spaces to suit her husband. Never built on since the area was subdivided in 1928, the lot sits among bungalow-sized houses whose owners wanted to be sure that the new design would fit in. "I was careful with the massing not to overwhelm the street," Dale notes.

A low, horizontal line is artfully held through the use of multiple front gables, a stepped-back second story, and a ten-foot-deep wraparound veranda. The sloping land behind visually swallows a garage and a finished basement. Inside the 3,400-square-foot, four-bedroom house, a serene wood-paneled foyer opens left onto the formal living and dining rooms or right into the great room, which extends across the house's width from the hearth to the kitchen. A master suite occupies the back of the house, removed from the children's rooms upstairs.

Even before Stewart hired a general contractor (Stanley Martin Companies), he located a cabinetmaker (Carriage Hill Cabinet and Millwork) to flesh out his modern interpretation of Greene and Greene woodwork, a college interest. The effect is as embracing as being in an old bungalow but as open as a space designed by Frank Lloyd Wright, its large spans freed up by modern materials. Commented Heather McCune, editor in chief of *Professional Builder,* which featured this 2001 Home of the Year winner: "We see this house as representing where new home design needs to go . . . smaller spaces with finer finishes."

Beyond the dining room and the kitchen, a Greene and Greene–style stairway, overlooking the great room, is the pivot point of the first floor (opposite). Furnishings include Basset and Lexington pieces and a Bradbury and Bradbury frieze in the dining room. ▪ Warm green and brown tones were chosen to blend the house into its environment of mature trees and shrubs (top). The columns are cedar, but the piers are concrete molded to mimic stone, the exterior is clad in hard-wearing cementitous siding, and the trim is polyvinyl chloride. ▪ For the house's interior built-ins and trim, Dale Stewart returned to the Arts and Crafts movement's preferred quartersawn oak (above). That some units hold CDs and videotapes and that the fireplace is fashioned of concrete attests to his skillful melding of old and new.

Sheer Poetry

Whittier Place in the Takoma neighborhood of Washington is a short street long on bungalows. Named for the poet John Greenleaf Whittier (1807–92), it is somewhat of an anomaly amidst streets calling to mind trees—Aspen, Butternut, Cedar, Holly, Willow—in this in-town garden suburb. But Whittier, an antiwar Quaker abolitionist who became a "household poet," fit well into the progressive psyche of Takoma Park then and now.

One of Takoma's residents in 1917 was Harry H. Bugbee, a clerk for the Navy Department. His impressive frame bungalow on Whittier Place was designed by an architect who had opened his office only a few years previously. George T. Santmyers (1889–1960) soon went on to become "the most prolific architect of Washington apartment buildings in the history of the city," according to the historian James Goode. With paired dormers above paired windows, the house exhibits pleasing symmetry.

It has taken Faith Wheeler and her family more than two and a half decades to revive the two-bedroom, 3,700-square-foot bungalow. She wanted a fixer-upper in a stable urban neighborhood, thinking that she "could preserve everything. But that was a pipe dream!" she adds. "The house was in dire need of repair when we bought it." On the list of disasters were the heating system, a leaky roof, creaky floors, broken windows, cracked plaster, a damp basement, and gold aluminum siding that was "dented, discolored, and generally ugly."

First to be remodeled was the kitchen, where a breakfast bay was added to frame lovely fruit trees in the back yard. The plaster walls could not be salvaged. She was luckier when it came to removing the siding, which hid shingles in good condition—brown, and probably dark green before that—that have since been given a new coat of paint.

The work took its toll on the family: life-threatening illness in Wheeler's daughter, a long separation between husband and wife, temporary relocation during the upstairs renovation, and some work unfinished for years. Both family and bungalow are now back on track. "Restoring this place has been quite a journey, with many twists and turns, some of which I wish had never happened." But, adds this daughter and niece of builders and developers, "The house is looking like I thought it always would."

Faith Wheeler's home, which cost $3,000 in 1917, is wider than most bungalows on Whittier Place but at 28 feet deep is relatively shallow (opposite, top). The broad porch, which first attracted her to the house, stands out against the newly painted shingles. Wheeler wanted a cheerier color than the original brown. "I'm partial to water, so aqua worked for me," she says. ▪ Just inside the front door, built-in cabinets separate the living and dining rooms (bottom). Off the living room is a study with new French doors, a product of Wheeler's goal to bring more light into the living room and generally increase the illusion of spaciousness. An au pair suite was added in the basement.

Safari Style

For an army veterinarian who has twice climbed Mount Kilimanjaro, tackling the renovation of a bungalow in Washington's historic Takoma neighborhood was a comparatively easy challenge. After Major Howard Gobble, D.V.M., returned to the States from ten years spent administering animal vaccine programs in East Africa, he found this "cozy but not crowded" bungalow close to Walter Reed Army Medical Center. It had been vacant for several years, but earlier tenants had left an oily trail—after running their motorcycles up and into the living room. Despite this, he says, "It had a warm, welcoming feel. I was surprised at how open it was, how the space flowed."

The frame house, with its low shed roof and broad front porch, was designed by G. W. Chase, a local builder, and constructed in 1926 for Dorothy and Martin Elenbaum, who later became an auditor for the Navy Department. For $6,000 they got a house that almost fills its 40-foot-wide lot side to side. After Gobble upgraded the plumbing and electrical systems, reroofed the house, redid the plaster walls in the dining room, and stripped and refinished the hardwood pine floors and trim, he built more living space in what was originally an 1,800-square-foot house. Both the attic and the basement were finished, adding three new bedrooms and bathrooms. The glass knobs on the French doors needed only cleaning.

Now the veterinarian has left his own mark on the house, which is filled with elephants, camels, giraffes, and other reminders of his work to save African animals. A Red Sea tortoise shell in the living room was found at a landfill in Djibouti. "It's simple and comfortable," he reflects about his bungalow, "humble yet not embarrassing."

Six tall windows facing the porch as well as sidelights alongside the offset front door bring generous light into what was originally a two-bedroom house (below). ▪ Four tall, squared posts support the porch roof (opposite, top). Wide-spaced muntins and mullions reflect the later construction date. ▪ In the airy front bedroom overlooking the porch, a leather elephant from a market in Addis Ababa sits atop an Arts and Crafts–style desk (bottom).

Painted "Beyond Red," the dining room show-cases a 1918 Arts and Crafts sideboard and a pine farm table bought at auction. On the table are two *bunna* stools carried by Ethiopians to sit on whenever the occasion arises (left). ▪ The owner's collections reflect his life in Africa. The Kenyan giraffe sculpture was carved from an acacia tree (above). Beneath a bowl holding a white ostrich egg, an East African camel recalls the veterinarian's treatment of camels in Kenya.

Bungalow Olé

||n the "sylvan suburb" of Takoma, scientists and government workers were invited to become landed gentry. E. O. Ulrick, an archaeologist with the Smithsonian Institution, accepted the challenge, hiring D. L. Richardson in 1923 to design a bungalow for himself and his wife, an opera singer, along the trolley line. A few years earlier the Panama-California Exposition of 1915, held in San Diego, had sparked a national love affair with Spanish architecture. The result here in Takoma was an unusual oversized bungalow with a twist of old Spain.

At a time when average bungalows were selling for $5,000, the Ulrick home on its corner lot cost about $20,000 (plus $800 for a garage, both built by G. W. Chase). Inside, it is easy to see why. Many of the original furnishings—custom made to suit the family's German heritage—remain in place, respectfully preserved by succeeding owners. A mahogany sideboard in the dining room too heavy to move, original wallpaper, even an ancient refrigerator and rotary telephone help create a stage set now lovingly cared for by Marcella and Terry Jones. "When my daughter and I walked in," remembers Marcella, an active community volunteer, "it felt like we had just gotten a big hug."

Upstairs, "It was like a window opening up." For here, filling much of the upper floor, is a large ballroom in which Mrs. Ulrick reportedly gave concerts. Takoma had welcomed its very first theater and community auditorium about two blocks away in the same year the house was built. After nearly a decade here, adding amenities such as a sauna and an indoor pool, the Joneses decided to return the ballroom space to its intended purpose by creating a theater of their own up in paradise.

With its stucco walls and hipped roof of red tile, the house is not unlike a bungalow offered by the Radford Architectural Company in 1908 (top). Three bedrooms are on the first floor, two on the second, and one in the finished basement. ▪ The old radio is a symbolic holdover: Terry Jones's company provides venture capital to develop minority radio, television, and cable ownership (center). ▪ The original wood-paneled Frigidaire, powered by a motor in the basement, still has its instruction booklet (bottom). ▪ Crystal is embedded in Sheamus Shamus's swan window added over the fireplace (opposite). The previous owners would sell only to a buyer they felt sure would preserve the house and its contents.

Home Again

Houses, like neighborhoods, metamorphose over time, evolving into a palimpsest whose layers of history can be read by those interested enough to look. In Takoma Park, Maryland—Takoma's sister city just over the District line—Art McMurdie, a developer-builder, looked around at once respectable bungalows whose virtues had become lost over the years and saw that they could make happy homes again. Kathy Brooks-Denny, a past resident of Takoma Park who had remained secretary of Historic Takoma, came calling one recent New Year's Day in search of a bungalow of her own. When her husband, Robert L. Denny II, caught sight of the bungalow McMurdie was renovating, previously divided into five apartments by the next-door owners, he exclaimed: "There's no way I'm buying that house!"

"It was a complete mess," she admits. The back was wide open, an earlier addition having been removed, and the 1918 bungalow was wrapped in lime green asbestos shingles. But she knew that McMurdie had been honored for his work in renovating Takoma Park's historic houses. Buying before the renovation was completed allowed the couple to shape some of the remaining design, guided by the architect Paul Treseder and inspired by ideas in publications such as *American Bungalow.*

To the right of the door they made a former bedroom into a library, where Bob now has a ledge atop the bookcases for his train collection and Kathy has a two-level built-in rabbit condo housing rescued rabbits before they are adopted. Upstairs in the 2,500-square-foot bungalow is a new master suite, one of three bedrooms. They carved a wine cellar out of the root cellar, and a butler's pantry by the dining room is planned. Once a week now, Bob tells Kathy how much he loves the house.

Battered piers covered with deep red shingles support the full-width porch (opposite, top left). With its gabled dormer punctuating the shed roof, the house would be the Washington bungalow archetype if not for its rare pebbledash stucco finish. ▪ The fireplace in the new family room at the back of the house was designed by Paul Treseder to display Pratt and Larson tiles (top right). Squirrels, acorns, and rabbits are immortalized in tile. ▪ Everything beyond the dining room is new, including an open gourmet kitchen with red birch cabinets and green marble counters (bottom left). At the back a sunny breakfast nook overlooks a new porch and a deep back yard. ▪ The tub comes from the original house, but the period-style bathroom downstairs had to be rebuilt around it (bottom right). ▪ Although the front door is original, the pebbledash stucco had been neglected too long to be salvaged (above). The owners happened on a craftsman in Alexandria, Virginia, who knew how to mix the gray and white pebbles in concrete, a labor-intensive process.

Selected Bibliography

Books

Cigliano, Jan. *Bungalow.* American Restoration Style Series. Layton, Utah: Gibbs Smith, 1998.

Comstock, William Phillips, and Clarence Eaton Schermerhorn. *Bungalows, Camps and Mountain Houses.* 1908; rev. 1915. Reprint, Washington, D.C.: American Institute of Architects Press, 1990.

Connolly, M. Caren, and Louis Wasserman. *Updating Classic America: Bungalows.* Newtown, Conn.: Taunton Press, 2002.

King, Anthony D. *The Bungalow: The Production of a Global Culture.* 1984. 2d ed. New York: Oxford University Press, 1995.

Kreisman, Lawrence. *Made to Last: Historic Preservation in Seattle and King County.* Historic Seattle Preservation Foundation. Seattle: University of Washington Press, 1999.

Lancaster, Clay. *The American Bungalow, 1880–1930.* 1985. Reprint, New York: Dover Publications, 1995.

Makinson, Randell L. *Greene and Greene: Architecture as a Fine Art.* Layton, Utah: Gibbs Smith, 1977.

Marsh, Ellen, and Mary Anne O'Boyle. *Takoma Park: Portrait of a Victorian Suburb, 1883–1983.* Takoma Park, Md.: Historic Takoma, 1984.

McGuckian, Eileen S. *Rockville: Portrait of a City.* Franklin, Tenn.: Hillsboro Press, 2001.

Ochsner, Jeffrey Karl, ed. *Shaping Seattle Architecture: A Historical Guide to the Architects.* American Institute of Architects Seattle Chapter and Seattle Architectural Foundation. Seattle: University of Washington Press, 1994.

Pacyga, Dominic A., and Charles Shanabruch, eds. *The Chicago Bungalow.* Chicago Architecture Foundation. Chicago: Arcadia Publishing, 2001.

Radford Architectural Company. *Radford's Artistic Bungalows: The Complete 1908 Catalog.* 1908. Reprint, New York: Dover Publications, 1997.

Schweitzer, Robert. *Bungalow Colors: Exteriors.* Layton, Utah: Gibbs Smith, 2002.

Smith, Bruce. *Greene and Greene: Masterworks.* San Francisco: Chronicle Books, 1998.

Smith, Kathryn Schneider, ed. *Washington at Home: An Illustrated History of Neighborhoods in the Nation's Capital.* Northridge, Calif.: Windsor Publications, 1988.

Stevenson, Katherine Cole, and H. Ward Jandl. *Houses by Mail: A Guide to Houses from Sears, Roebuck and Company.* Washington, D.C.: Preservation Press, 1986.

Stickley, Gustav. *Craftsman Homes: Architecture and Furnishings of the American Arts and Crafts Movement.* 1909. Reprint, New York: Dover Publications, 1979.

Stickley, Gustav, ed. *Craftsman Bungalows: 59 Homes from "The Craftsman."* 1903–16. Reprint, New York: Dover Publications, 1988.

Wilson, Henry L. *California Bungalows of the Twenties.* Reprint, New York: Dover Publications, 1993.

Winter, Robert. *American Bungalow Style.* New York: Simon and Schuster, 1996.

———. *The California Bungalow.* California Architecture and Architects Series, no. 1. Los Angeles: Hennessey and Ingalls, 1980.

Winter, Robert, ed. *Toward a Simpler Way of Life: The Arts and Crafts Architects of California.* Berkeley: University of California Press, 1997.

Wright, Gwendolyn. *Moralism and the Model Home: Domestic Architecture and Cultural Conflict in Chicago, 1873–1913.* Chicago: University of Chicago Press, 1980.

Articles and Reports

Andersen, Tim. "Twenty Years Later: Revisiting the Heinemans' Finest Bungalow." *American Bungalow,* no. 25, spring 2000.

Basye, Alison. "Mixed Company." *Seattle,* October 2000.

Bowler, Molly. "Easy Living, Chicago Style." *American Bungalow,* no. 3, 1990.

Bungalow Heaven Neighborhood Association, Home Tour Notes, 2000, 2002.

Counts, Tim. "Creating a Classic Bungalow Kitchen." *American Bungalow,* no. 30, summer 2001.

———. "The Affordable Bungalow Interior." *American Bungalow,* no. 16, winter 1997.

Dean, Patty. "It Is Here We Live: Minneapolis Homes and the Arts and Crafts Movement." *Minnesota History,* spring 2001.

Elliott, Lynn. "Bungalow Built-ins." *Old-House Journal,* September-October 1994.

Gringeri-Brown, Michelle. "The All-American Bungalow." *American Bungalow,* no. 30, summer 2001.

———. "At Home with American Bungalow: Exterior Paint Challenges." *American Bungalow,* no. 28, winter 2000.

———. "Bungalow on a Bluff." *American Bungalow,* no. 32, winter 2001.

———. "Converts to New Construction." *American Bungalow,* no. 35, fall 2002.

———. "A Great Time for Bungalows." *American Bungalow,* no. 35, fall 2002.

———. "Saving Homes Block by Block." *American Bungalow,* no. 36, winter 2002.

Hoppin, Ted, and Anne Sommer. "Re-Creating Yesterday with Today's Materials." *American Bungalow,* no. 25, spring 2000.

Johnson, Kristi Lee. "The Twin Cities Bungalow Club Finds a Home." *American Bungalow,* no. 22, summer 1999.

Kreisman, Lawrence. "Cabin in the Woods." *American Bungalow,* no. 30, summer 2001.

———. "Denny Blaine Storey." *Pacific Northwest (Seattle Times* Magazine), April 12, 1998.

Luke, John. "Southwest Bungalow—High on a Hill." *American Bungalow,* no. 29, spring 2001.

Reichardt, Mary. "In St. Paul, Bungalows Are Back." *American Bungalow,* no. 22, summer 1999.

Simpson, David, and Janice Griffin. "The Workingman's Bungalow." *American Bungalow,* no. 3, 1990.

Traceries, Inc. Historic Structure Report on the Hier-Myhre Residence, Washington, D.C.

Villa Historic Committee. *The Villa, 1907–1997.* Chicago: Villa Improvement League, 1997.

Wenger, Loralee. "Everything Old Is New Again." *Renovation Style,* winter 1997.

Williams, Michael. "The Bungalows of Chicago's Far North Side." *American Bungalow,* no. 32, winter 2001.

Williams, Michael, and Michelle Gringeri-Brown. "Chicago Does It Right." *American Bungalow,* no. 29, spring 2001.

Winter, Robert. "Arthur S. and Alfred Heineman." *American Bungalow,* no. 8, 1994.

———. The Weaver House: Architecture Notes. n.d.

Resources

Organizations

CHICAGO

Chicago Architecture Foundation
224 South Michigan Avenue
Suite 430
Chicago, IL 60604
voice: 312-922-3432
www.architecture.org

Historic Chicago Bungalow Initiative
c/o Historic Chicago Bungalow Association
1 North LaSalle Street
12th Floor
Chicago, IL 60602
voice: 312-642-9900
fax: 312-360-0758
www.chicagobungalow.org

Neighborhood Housing Services of Chicago
11001 South Michigan Avenue
Chicago, IL 60628
voice: 773-568-1020
fax: 773-928-0241
www.nhschicago.org

LOS ANGELES – PASADENA

American Bungalow Magazine
P.O. Box 756
Sierra Madre, CA 91025-0756
voice: 800-350-3363
www.ambungalow.com

Bungalow Heaven Neighborhood Association
P.O. Box 40812
Pasadena, CA 91114-7672
voice: 626-585-2172
http://home.earthlink.net/~bhna

Gamble House
4 Westmoreland Place
Pasadena, CA 91103
voice: 626-793-3334
www.gamblehouse.org

Los Angeles Conservancy
523 West Sixth Street
Suite 826
Los Angeles, CA 90014
voice: 213-623-2489
fax: 213-623-3909
www.laconservancy.org
info@laconservancy.org

Pasadena Heritage
651 South St. John Avenue
Pasadena, CA 91105-2913
voice: 626-441-6333
fax: 626-441-2917
www.pasadenaheritage.org

MINNEAPOLIS – ST. PAUL

Twin Cities Bungalow Club
c/o Tim Counts, President
3547 24th Avenue South
Minneapolis, MN 55406
voice: 612-724-5816
www.mtn.org/bungalow
bungalowclub@hotmail.com

SEATTLE

Historic Seattle
1117 Minor Avenue
Seattle, WA 98101
voice: 206-622-6952
fax: 206-622-1197
www.historicseattle.org
info@historicseattle.org

Seattle Neighborhood History
www.historylink.org

WASHINGTON, D.C.

Alexandria Historical Society
The Lyceum
201 South Washington St.
Alexandria, VA 22314
voice: 703-838-4994

Arlington Historical Society
P.O. Box 402
Arlington, VA 22210
voice: 703-892-4204
www.arlingtonhistoricalsociety.org
info@arlingtonhistoricalsociety.org

Historic Takoma
P.O. Box 5781
Takoma Park, MD 20913
voice: 301-270-2831
www.historictakoma.org
info@historictakoma.org

Historical Society of Washington, D.C.
City Museum of Washington, D.C.
801 K Street, NW
Washington, DC 20001
voice: 202-383-1800
www.hswdc.org
www.citymuseumdc.org
info@citymuseumdc.org

Peerless Rockville
29 Courthouse Square
Room 110
Rockville, MD 20850
voice: 301-762-0096
www.peerlessrockville.org

Architects and Designers

CHICAGO

Doug Farr
Farr Associates
53 West Jackson Street
Suite 1661
Chicago, IL 60604
voice: 312-408-1661
www.farrside.com
doug@farrside.com

Daniel J. Ford
Greene and Proppe
   Design
1209 West Berwyn Avenue
Chicago, IL 60640
voice: 773-271-1925
fax: 773-271-1936
www.gpdchicago.com

Scott Sonoc and Bruce
   Klein
Sonoc Architects and
   Associates
735 West Division Street
Chicago, IL 60610
voice: 312-266-5954
fax: 312-266-5968
www.sonoc.com
sonoc@sonoc.com

MINNEAPOLIS – ST. PAUL

David Herreid
Wichser and Herreid
   Architects
3476 Lake Elmo Avenue
   North
Lake Elmo, MN 55042
voice: 651-777-7054
fax: 651-777-5931
www.finelinearchitecture.
   com
design@w-harchitects.
   com

Joe Metzler
SALA Architects
43 Main Street, SE
Suite 410
Minneapolis, MN 55414
voice: 612-379-3037
fax: 612-379-0001
www.salaarc.com

SEATTLE

Tim Andersen
7726 33d Avenue, NE
Seattle, WA 98115
voice: 206-524-8841
www.TJAndersen.com
timsen@comcast.net

Curtis Gelotte Architects
150 Lake Street South
Suite 208
Kirkland, WA 98033
voice: 425-828-3081
fax: 425-822-2152
www.gelotte.com
info@gelotte.com

Christian Gladu
The Bungalow Company
P.O. Box 584
Bend, OR 97709
voice: 800-945-9206
fax: 877-785-7512
www.thebungalow
   company.com
info@thebungalow
   company.com

Alexandra Gorny
Wai/Gorny
1029 N.E. 62d Street
Seattle, WA 98115
voice: 206-523-8125
fax: 206-985-0273
www.waigorny.com

Joseph Greif Architects
921 N.E. Boat Street
Seattle, WA 98105
voice: 206-633-4293
fax: 206-633-3735
www.josephgreifarchitects.
   com
greif@msn.com

Karen Hovde
Interior Vision in the
   Craftsman Style
23 Oak Shore Court
Port Townsend, WA 98368
voice: 888-385-3161
www.interiorvision.com
karen@interiorvision.com

Larry Johnson and
   Howard Miller
The Johnson Partnership
1212 N.E. 65th Street
Seattle, WA 98115
voice: 206-523-1618
fax: 206-523-9786
www.tjp.us
larry@thejohnson
   partnership.com

Mary and Ray Johnston
Johnston Architects
3503 N.E. 45th Street
Suite 2
Seattle, WA 98105
voice: 206-523-6150
fax: 206-523-9382
www.johnstonarchitects.
   com
jarch@johnstonarchitects.
   com

Ann Landis
Olympic Design Group
606 Roosevelt
Port Townsend, WA 98368
voice: 800-490-9070
fax: 360-385-5614
www.morganhilldesign.
   com
odg@morganhilldesign.
   com

David and Irving
   Spellman
Spellman Construction
8509 Ferncliff Avenue
Bainbridge Island, WA
   98110
voice: 206-842-2786
www.angelfire.com/falcon/
   spellman/index2/html
spellcon@blarg.com

Laurie Taylor
Ivy Hill Interiors
3920 S.W. 109th Street
Seattle, WA 98146
voice: 206-243-6768
ltaylor@mx.serv.net

Daniel R. Yarger Design
1449 N.E. 120th Street
Seattle, WA 98125
voice: 206-363-5698
fax: 206-524-6911

WASHINGTON, D.C.

Mark Goldsborough
Goldsborough Design
   Build
18956 Bonanza Way
Gaithersburg, MD 20879
voice: 301-721-1900
fax: 301-721-9899
mark.goldsborough
   @earthlink.net

Michael Holt/Architects
1701 N Street, NW
Washington, DC 20036
voice: 202-234-4972
michaelholt.mha
   @verizon.net

Art McMurdie
Cleveland Avenue
   Development
12 Cleveland Avenue
Takoma Park, MD 20912
voice: 301-565-0524
fax: 301-565-5961

Dale A. Stewart, AIA
CORE
1010 Wisconsin
   Avenue, NW
Suite 405
Washington, DC 20007
voice: 202-466-6116
fax: 202-466-6235
www.coredc.com
gen@coredc.com

Paul Treseder Architect
6320 Wiscasset Road
Bethesda, MD 20816
voice: 301-320-1580
paul.treseder@verizon.net

James Viviano
131 Frontenac Forest
Frontenac, MO 63131
voice: 314-997-6012
jamesviviano@aol.com